POSTAL WORKER EXAM

POSTAL
WORKER
EXAM

Fourth Edition

LEARNING EXPRESS ®

NEW YORK

Library of Congress Cataloging-in-Publication Data:
Postal worker exam—4th ed.
  p. cm.
  ISBN-13: 978-1-57685-675-8
  ISBN-10: 1-57685-675-5
 1. Postal service—United States—Examinations, questions, etc. I.
LearningExpress (Organization)
  HE6499.P655 2009
  383'.1076—dc22

                                                    2008037034

Printed in the United States of America

9 8 7 6 5 4 3 2 1

ISBN 13 978-1-57685-675-8

For information on LearningExpress, other LearningExpress products, or bulk sales, please write to us at:
  LearningExpress
  2 Rector Street
  26th Floor
  New York, NY 10006

Or visit us at:
  www.learnatest.com

Contents

INTRODUCTION	How to Use This Book	ix
CHAPTER 1	About the USPS and Test 473	1
CHAPTER 2	Test 473 Content	19
CHAPTER 3	The LearningExpress Test Preparation System	25
CHAPTER 4	Practice Postal Worker Exam 1	39
CHAPTER 5	Address Checking Review	67
CHAPTER 6	Forms Completion Review	75
CHAPTER 7	Coding and Memory Review	83
CHAPTER 8	Personal Characteristics and Experience Inventory Review and Questions	97
CHAPTER 9	Practice Postal Worker Exam 2	115
CHAPTER 10	Practice Postal Worker Exam 3	141
CHAPTER 11	Practice Postal Worker Exam 4	167

Contributors

Eileen F. Brennan is an editor with Anton Community Newspapers on Long Island. She is the recipient of New York State journalism awards for local reporting.

Virginia Brennan, PhD, Adjunct Assistant Professor of Linguistics at Vanderbilt University, is a writer and editor living in Nashville, Tennessee.

Susan Camardo is a business and careers writer and communications consultant based in New York City.

Elizabeth Chesla, MA, is an adult educator and curriculum developer in New York City, and has also taught reading and writing.

Sandy Gade is a freelance writer and editor based in San Diego, California.

Judith F. Olson, MA, is a chairperson of the language arts department at Valley High School in West Des Moines, Iowa, where she also conducts test-preparation workshops.

Judith Robinovitz is an independent educational consultant and director of Score At the Top, a comprehensive test-preparation program in Vero Beach, Florida.

Hilda Speicher has a PhD in Social Psychology and is an Assistant Professor of Psychology at Albertus Magnus College in New Haven, Connecticut. Formerly, Dr. Speicher worked in the pharmaceutical marketing research industry and for a mental health advocacy group doing research on best practices and program evaluation.

Shirley Tarbell is a test development specialist and writer living in Portland, Maine.

Introduction: How to Use This Book ▶

We want you to get the most you can out of this book to ensure that you get the score you need for the job you want. This comprehensive book contains information about job opportunities with the United States Postal Service (USPS), information about the exam you will take, tips on preparing for test day, review chapters for each part of the exam, as well as four full-length practice tests. Armed with this amount of information, you are preparing yourself to succeed. Here is how each chapter of this book works.

In **Chapter 1**, you will learn about the history, organization, and services of the USPS. You will also find information about the types of jobs available as well as the salaries and benefits you can expect as an employee.

Chapter 2 offers an overview on a USPS job search and an introduction to the format and content of Test 473, also referred to in this book as the Postal Worker Exam.

Once you know about the types of jobs available and the exam you need to take, you can start our exclusive LearningExpress Test Preparation System in **Chapter 3**. The nine steps in this chapter will help you get in top physical and mental shape for test day.

In **Chapter 4**, you will find the first full-length practice test. You should use this test to diagnose your strengths and weaknesses, so you can focus your preparation on the types of questions that give you the most difficulty.

In **Chapters 5 through 8**, you can review all the material that is covered on the Postal Worker Exam. Each chapter reviews a different part of the test.

Finally, **Chapters 9 through 11** contain three additional full-length practice tests, complete with answer keys for each section. You should use these tests to gauge your improvement as well as to target which areas you need to review with particular care.

About the USPS and Test 473

CHAPTER SUMMARY

Congratulations on taking the first step toward a career with the United States Postal Service (USPS). This chapter offers you information on the history, organization, and services of the USPS. You will also learn the job descriptions for several positions as well as the hiring process potential employees must complete. Specifically, you will learn some of the ways you can find USPS job openings that require you to take Test 473, the Postal Worker Exam.

As someone who is thinking about working with the USPS, you may find its history particularly interesting. The USPS has a long and fascinating history that began, of all places, in a bar. Yes, that's right—the very first "post office" in the colonies was Richard Fairbanks's Tavern in Boston, Massachusetts.

▶ USPS History

In 1639, Richard Fairbanks's Tavern became the first official repository for overseas mail. This may sound odd to us today, but at the time, using a tavern as a post office wasn't an unusual practice; this is how mail was generally distributed in England and other parts of Europe. It wasn't until almost 50 years later (1683) that the first official post office was established in Pennsylvania by William Penn. In the South, on the other hand, most mail was delivered not by way of post offices or taverns, but by messengers (often slaves) who ran mail between the plantations.

Postal service in the colonies was centralized in 1691, but service was lackluster until Benjamin Franklin was appointed Joint Postmaster General for the Crown in 1737. He reorganized the system and improved postal routes, thereby dramatically improving mail service. Under Franklin's tenure, the colonial mail system had its first profitable year. As the Revolutionary War neared, however, Franklin was fired for his support of the rebellious colonies. But by the time he was dismissed, he had established 30 post offices in the Northeast.

Mail Service in the Colonies

When the colonies started to break away from England, the Continental Congress—first organized in May 1775—met to address the needs of the new nation they were forming. One of its primary concerns was the mail, and on July 26, 1775, Benjamin Franklin became the first Postmaster General of the new Post Office Department (POD). In just over a year, Franklin devised the Post Office Department system that remains the core of our country's mail service today.

Mail Delivery in the United States

Today, we have many options for sending and receiving mail, which is delivered by truck, train, plane, and on foot. But there weren't always so many choices, and some of the ways mail is delivered—means of transportation we now take for granted—have the POD and the USPS to thank for their advancement.

The USPS delivers mail directly to 141 million addresses. It does this six days a week. Much of it still moves by foot, but this is just one of many means by which mail has been delivered. Mail has traveled by horse, by stagecoach, by steamboat, by railroad, by automobile, and by airplane, as well as by balloon, by helicopter, and even, on one occasion, by missile.

The Pony Express

Perhaps the best known means of early mail delivery is the Pony Express. While the West was first being settled and during the years of the Gold Rush (which began in 1849), mail to the West Coast had to travel by boat to Panama, cross that country by train, and then move by boat up to California. Mail rarely reached its destination in less than a month. In fact, it often took months for it to reach the West Coast.

There had to be a better way, and entrepreneur William Russell thought he had the answer. So, in 1860, he published an ad that ran:

Wanted: Young, skinny, wiry fellows not over 18. Must be expert riders willing to risk death daily. Orphans preferred.

Thus began the Pony Express, a system of horses and riders that delivered mail across the continent in fewer than two weeks. Although it went out of business in late 1861 when the transcontinental telegraph line was completed, the Pony Express lives on in legend.

Rail and Rural Delivery

Meanwhile, mail was being increasingly delivered by rail, and much of it was actually sorted right on the trains. These trains became known as "post offices on wheels." For almost a century, from 1860 to 1950, railways were the main way of transporting mail.

Through mail delivery, the POD helped make major advances and improvements in transportation, aviation, and business in the United States. For example, unlike city residents, farmers and other rural residents used to have to travel—sometimes a whole day—to pick up their mail at their "local" post office. When they finally began to receive free rural delivery in 1896, roads and bridges, which were often crude and dangerous, had to be improved so that mail could be delivered properly. Free rural delivery was therefore central to rural development and to relieving the isolation of farmers.

Parcel post (package delivery), which became available in 1913, had a tremendous impact on the economy and led to the development and explosion of mail-order houses. The first of these was the famous Montgomery Ward, whose catalogs were considered "bibles" by the rurally isolated farmers. Sears, Roebuck and Company tripled its revenues with just five years of parcel post service.

Aviation Advancements

It's actually in aviation that the POD may have had the most profound effect. Sensing not only the feasibility but the practicality of mail transportation by air, the POD encouraged experimental flights for mail delivery. The first was in 1911, between Garden City and Mineola, New York. Then, the POD enlisted the Army Signal Corps, whose students got to practice their flying while delivering the mail. Soon, regular flights were delivering mail between New York and Washington.

But early planes were primitive, and safety measures and features were nearly nonexistent. Landing fields, towers, searchlights, lighted instrument panels, navigational lights, and other safety features and measures we now take for granted were implemented largely at the impetus of the POD, which was concerned for the safety of its pilots and the efficiency of its delivery program. In fact, the POD contributed so much to the development of aviation safety that in 1922, 1923, and 1926, the POD received awards for its contributions to aeronautics.

By 2008, commercial airlines carried 10.5 million pounds of mail, six days a week.

Evolution of Efficiency

Because the transportation of mail was becoming more efficient, mail sorting and processing had to improve as well. Here are some of the ways the POD met this challenge to make the USPS what it is today.

ZIP Codes

In 2008, the USPS handled more than 202 billion pieces of mail. Because of the dramatic increase in mail volume and the evolution of transportation in the first half of the 20th century, the POD had to develop a more efficient way of sorting and delivering mail. The solution? ZIP (Zoning Improvement Plan) codes, which went into effect in 1963. This five-digit system allows sorters to pinpoint the location of addressees. The first digit in the ZIP code, for example, indicates one of nine zones across the United States (0 in the Northeast, 9 in the far West). The second and third digits identify increasingly specific regions within that zone and the last two numbers indicate the local post office. In 1983, the USPS introduced the ZIP+4, which includes the standard five-digit code, followed by four more numbers. Although not mandatory, including the ZIP+4 directs mail to specific city blocks, buildings, and other recipients.

Reorganization

The 1960s were a turbulent and troubled era for the POD. Mail volume was increasing but efficiency was not, despite the new ZIP codes. There was also labor trouble, and in 1966, the Chicago Post Office was so backlogged with mail that it was unable to function. An ensuing labor strike across the nation led to a much-needed Postal Reorganization Act, which went into effect in August 1970. This reorganization officially separated the POD from the Congress, and the POD became the new United States Postal Service (USPS), an independent part of the executive branch of the government. The reorganization gave the USPS the structure it has today and instituted regulations for employees, labor management, transportation, finances, and rates.

Mechanization

Later in the 1970s, the USPS began an important era of mechanization by introducing the optical character reader (OCR). The first OCRs read the address on a letter one line at a time and printed a corresponding barcode on the envelope. Then, a barcode sorter (BCS) read the barcode and sorted the envelope accordingly. These machines automated much of the sorting process and decreased sorting time dramatically.

The single-line OCRs of the late 1970s were replaced by fast multiple-line OCRs (MLOCRs), which can read an entire address and apply the appropriate barcode in milliseconds. Handwritten or difficult to read mail was sorted out and handled by remote barcoding systems (RBCSs), which send an image of the envelope to an operator at another site. The operator read the address, input the correct information, and sent it back to the RBCS, which then applied an appropriate barcode.

Since 1999, robots have been used to sort mail and load it for transportation. Most recently, cameras have replaced barcode readers. The use of these cameras also allows the USPS to track a piece of mail from its receipt to its delivery.

Online Services

Because of increases in competition from other mail carriers and improvements in technology, the USPS has been using the Internet to meet customer needs for convenience, flexibility, and profitability.

Here are just a few of the services that are available online. Customers can:

- find a ZIP code
- calculate postage
- locate a post office
- track and confirm packages
- schedule mail pickup
- print a shipping label
- complete a Change of Address form
- buy stamps
- find out about international services

Before you leave the house for the post office, go online at www.usps.com to see if what you need can be done from your computer.

▶ Organizational Structure

Just as it's important to know what services the USPS offers, it's important to know how the USPS is organized.

Board of Governors

The USPS is governed by a Board of Governors, which is equivalent to the Board of Directors of a corporation. Nine governors are appointed by the president with the approval of Congress. Their nine-year terms are staggered, so one governor's term expires each year, and no more than five of these nine can be members of the same political party. These governors then select a Postmaster General, and together they select a Deputy Postmaster General. These eleven members form the governing board of the USPS, which directs the finances, policies, planning, and practices of the USPS.

Territory Divisions

The USPS has divided the United States into ten postal service areas. Each area has a manager of customer services and a processing and distribution manager. These ten areas are further divided into 85 local customer service districts.

▶ Services

The USPS currently offers a wide range of services to businesses and private customers. There are three classes of mail—first class, periodicals (formerly second class), and standard (formerly third and fourth class). First-class mail is generally delivered within two to three business days but can take as long as seven to ten days. For urgent mail, the USPS offers Express Mail (guaranteed next day delivery) and Priority Mail (within two to three days). There are even several international options offered. The fastest, Global Express Guaranteed, will have your package arriving within one to three days.

The USPS also offers dozens of other mailing services. Several of these services provide you with proof that your mail was sent and/or received. If you're sending a valuable package, you can send it Registered Mail, which means your package will be carefully guarded until it reaches its destination. You can also have valuable packages insured. Special Handling for packages that require special care (like live animals) and Special Delivery services are also available. And if you don't want mail sent to your home or office, the USPS will rent you a post office box and deliver all of your mail there for you to pick up at your convenience.

In addition, the USPS offers special services for customers and consumers. If a package has been lost, you can have it traced; if your insured, registered, COD (collect on delivery), or Express Mail has been damaged or lost, you can file a claim to recover your losses. If you suspect mail fraud, you can call the U.S. Postal Inspection Service, the law enforcement division of the USPS, which will investigate your complaint. You may also purchase money orders (up to $700) at post offices.

► Why Work for the USPS?

The USPS has more than 700,000 employees. It is one of the largest civilian employers in the United States. The USPS is an indispensable part of our society. Other industries may come and go, but mail service is essential.

Mail service is so important, in fact, that it was one of the very first organizations formed by the Continental Congress when the American colonies first sought independence from England. Every year since, as our country's population has grown and our technology has advanced, the USPS has expanded to meet the growing demands of the businesses and people of this country.

Salaries and Benefits

The USPS has dozens of entry-level jobs—and because of expansions, promotions, and retirements, tens of thousands of job vacancies open up each year. As a career employee, you'll enjoy regular raises and the opportunity to bid for some of the more than 2,000 job titles within the USPS. You'll also enjoy a competitive salary, even at the entry level. For more detailed salary information, see pages 9–11.

Because the USPS is a government agency, its benefits package is outstanding. Career employees receive:

- 10 paid holidays per year
- 13 paid sick days per year
- 13–26 paid vacation days per year
- life insurance
- health insurance
- government pension
- thrift savings plan (similar to 401(k))

In addition, career employees are backed by strong, successful unions, including the National Association of Letter Carriers (NALC), the National Postal Mail Handlers Union (NPMHU), the American Postal Workers Union (APWU), and the National Rural Letter Carriers Association (NRLCA), which negotiate for regular salary increases and cost of living adjustments as well as increasingly better working conditions for USPS employees.

Job Security and Steady Hiring

The USPS has never had a layoff. Although automation has made it possible for fewer people to do more work, hiring by the USPS generally remains steady. Recently, eligible employees were offered voluntary retirement options.

Employee Programs

The USPS offers its employees support in many ways. One of them is the Employee Assistance Program (EAP), which offers USPS employees and their families access to more than 15,000 experienced counselors throughout the United States. Help is available 24 hours per day, seven days per week. The EAP has teamed with the Office of Workplace Environment Improvement (WEI) to address employees' questions and concerns about Equal Employment Opportunity (EEO), sexual harassment, potential violence, as well as any other job-related issues.

The Environment and Safety

The USPS is actively involved in environmental protection measures, particularly recycling. It uses a large portion of recycled products, and many of its own products are made out of recycled materials. The USPS also experiments with alternative fuel vehicles. In fact, thousands of USPS vehicles operate on compressed natural gas.

The USPS is also concerned about employee safety. There is an increased number of inspections at its locations, and as a result, employee accidents have been significantly reduced. The USPS has also instituted measures to prevent injuries in the workplace from repetitive motion—an important concern for the large percentage of USPS employees who do physically repetitive work. In addition, USPS facilities are smoke-free environments.

In response to concerns about biochemical terrorism, the USPS has also worked to develop Biohazard Detection Systems (BDS) and Ventilation Filtration Systems (VFS) for the processing equipment that handles incoming mail.

Community Service

The USPS and its employees are active in community service. Each May, for example, the NALC holds an annual food drive. Since 1985, the USPS has also participated in ADVO, Inc.'s missing children campaign by circulating "Have You Seen Me" cards with pictures of missing children through the mail. Since the start of this program, 136 of those children have been found. These are just a few of the many ways the USPS is involved in the community.

▶ Employee Categories

USPS employees generally fall into four categories:

- Casual
- Part-time flexible
- Part-time regular
- Full-time regular

Let's look at each of these categories in more detail:

Casual employees are typically hired for 90 days at time. Casual employment is often required during especially busy periods, such as around holidays or during times in which vacation time is at a peak.

Part-time flexible employees do not have a guaranteed amount of hours, nor do they have a fixed work schedule. Part-time flexible employees are used on an "as needed" basis.

Part-time regular employees have fixed schedules of fewer than 40 hours per week. They often fill in for full-time employees.

Full-time regular employees work five days per week, 40 hours per week.

▶ Entry-Level Job Descriptions

Now let's take a look at the specific entry-level jobs that require you to take Test 473.

City carrier: City carriers deliver and collect mail to and from city businesses and residents. Carriers usually have a set route on which they deliver and collect mail, by foot or vehicle depending upon their area. They spend much of their time outdoors (in all weather conditions) and are alone and unsupervised. Some city carriers must carry a mailbag, which is nearly 35 pounds when full. Carriers also have to unload mail containers up to 70 pounds. Due to the nature of the work, city carriers spend long periods of time standing and walking. **Note:** City carriers must also have a current, valid state driver's license, two years of driving experience, and a clean driving record.

Mail processing clerk: Mail processing clerks sort mail manually as well as monitor automated processing equipment. They must organize, gather, and move processed mail. This job involves heavy lifting and transport.

Mail handler: Mail handlers load and unload mail from trucks and bins and help in the initial sorting phases. They are required to lift and move heavy containers (up to 70 pounds) throughout the workday.

Sales, services, and distribution associate:
Associates provide customer service and sell directly to the consumer. They work in a retail environment and must complete and pass a job training program.

Grades and Steps

The bulk of USPS positions are classified into a certain category, grade, and step. The grade and step for each position determines the salary. For full-time regular salary information, turn to page 9.

Raises

USPS employees are awarded raises, which include a COLA (cost-of-living adjustment), on a regular basis. Ten COLAs are now guaranteed under an agreement reached in 2008. The third adjustment effective March 15, 2008, for example, gave all mail handlers an additional $479 a year. This came to 23 cents per hour and was based on the National Consumer Index for Urban Wage Earners and Clerical Workers.

The salary schedule for most positions is broken down into 12 steps, with each step being further broken down into different steps (labeled BB through RC). Basically, the longer you are with the USPS, the more you will earn and the more benefits you will receive.

▶ The Hiring Process

You've learned the history, organization, and services of the USPS. You have also learned about some of the reasons to seek employment, as well as what types of jobs are available. You know you want the job, so what, then, is the hiring process?

The hiring process starts with a few eligibility requirements. You must:

- be at least 18 years old, or 16 years old with a high school diploma
- be a U.S. citizen or permanent resident alien
- have a basic competency in English
- register with the Selective Service if you are a male born after December 31, 1959

Other employment eligibility requirements will be covered later.

If you meet the previous requirements and are seeking a job as a city carrier, mail processing clerk, mail handler, or sales, services, and distribution associate, you will have to apply to take Test 473. Here are the other steps in the process.

1. The USPS announces Test 473 openings to fill a position of city carrier, mail processing clerk, mail handler, or sales, services, and distribution associate.
2. You apply for Test 473 online* or by calling the toll-free number found on the job announcement.
3. You are sent information on where and when the test is being given.
4. You take Test 473.
5. The National Test Center Administration scores your test.
6. If you pass, your name is placed on a hiring register in numerical order according to your score on the test. That means, the higher your score, the higher your name appears on the register and the better your chances of being hired. Veterans may receive added points on the test scores and selection priority. If you do not pass, you will be informed that you will not be considered for employment with the USPS.

---

* When applying for Test 473 online, applicants are required to answer approximately 15 questions about their interests and preferences relating to work. Although the answers to these questions do not affect selection, they are intended to determine an applicant's genuine interest in the position.

This is just the beginning of the hiring process. You still have other requirements to meet. Prior to appointment and employment, you will also have to undergo a suitability assessment. This requires that you must disclose your employment history, any military experience, and any criminal conviction history. You must also pass a urinalysis drug test and a medical assessment (to determine your fitness level and ability to perform the tasks required), in addition to any other personal interviews required. Finally, for positions requiring driving (city carrier), applicants must have a valid driver's license and a safe driving record.

Hiring from Within

Entry-level positions are only a few of the thousands of jobs available with the USPS. In an effort to make it easier for current full-time USPS employees to apply for transfer or for promotions, the USPS has provided this information online. USPS employees and can search for and apply for jobs within the USPS at its website (www.usps.com).

Other Positions with the USPS

Don't forget that Test 473 is given only to applicants for certain jobs (city carrier, mail processing clerk, mail handler, and sales, services, and distribution associate). If these jobs do not appeal to you, do more research into the various positions available with the USPS as well as the different exams those jobs require.

▶ Moving On

Now that you've had an overview of the USPS—how it works, how it began and evolved, how you would benefit as an employee, how you would be hired, and what you would be doing—it's time to talk about the test that stands between you and the job you want. Turn to Chapter 2 to learn about the exam.

PAY SCALE OF NATIONAL POSTAL MAIL HANDLERS UNION

FULL-TIME ANNUAL BASIC RATES EFFECTIVE MARCH 15, 2008

FULL-TIME REGULAR—LEVEL 4

STEP	YEARLY	HOURLY	BIWEEKLY	OVERTIME
AA	29,496	14.18	1,134.46	21.27
A	33,735	16.22	1,297.50	24.33
B	39,047	18.77	1,501.81	28.16
C	41,558	19.98	1,598.38	29.97
D	45,254	21.76	1,740.54	32.64
E	45,551	21.90	1,751.96	32.85
F	45,855	22.05	1,763.65	33.08
G	46,150	22.19	1,775.00	33.29
H	46,452	22.33	1,786.62	33.50
I	46,751	22.48	1,798.12	33.72
J	47,056	22.62	1,809.85	33.93
K	47,352	22.77	1,821.23	34.16
L	47,653	22.91	1,832.81	34.37
M	47,953	23.05	1,844.35	34.58
N	48,251	23.20	1,855.81	34.80
O	48,550	23.34	1,867.31	35.01
P	48,851	23.49	1,878.88	35.24

NOTE: These figures do not include a September 2008 COLA and a November general wage increase.

FULL-TIME REGULAR—LEVEL 5				
STEP	YEARLY	HOURLY	BIWEEKLY	OVERTIME
AA	30,988	14.90	1,191.85	22.35
A	35,229	16.94	1,354.96	25.41
B	40,905	19.67	1,573.27	29.51
C	43,486	20.91	1,672.54	31.37
D	45,982	22.11	1,768.54	33.17
E	46,304	22.26	1,780.92	33.39
F	46,631	22.42	1,793.50	33.63
G	46,947	22.57	1,805.65	33.86
H	47,272	22.73	1,818.15	34.10
I	47,598	22.88	1,830.69	34.32
J	47,918	23.04	1,843.00	34.56
K	48,240	23.19	1,855.38	34.79
L	48,559	23.35	1,867.65	35.03
M	48,886	23.50	1,880.23	35.25
N	49,209	23.66	1,892.65	35.49
O	49,529	23.81	1,904.96	35.72
P	49,851	23.97	1,917.35	35.96

PART-TIME REGULAR AND FLEXIBLE EMPLOYEES

HOURLY BASIC RATES—LEVEL 4

(PART-TIME REGULARS)		(PART-TIME FLEXIBLE)	
STEP	HOURLY	STEP	HOURLY
AA	14.88	AA	14.75
A	16.22	A	16.87
B	18.77	B	19.52
C	19.98	C	20.78
D	21.76	D	22.63
E	21.90	E	22.78
F	22.05	F	22.93
G	22.19	G	23.08
H	22.33	H	23.23
I	22.48	I	23.38
J	22.62	J	23.53
K	22.77	K	23.68
L	22.91	L	23.83
M	23.05	M	23.98
N	23.20	N	24.13
O	23.34	O	24.28
P	23.49	P	24.43

- Regularly check **local television, newspaper, and radio advertisements** for any hiring opportunities with the USPS.
- Contact any **community groups or organizations** in your area to see if they have been informed of upcoming job listings with the USPS.

▶ Online Job Listings

One of the most important things to know when looking for a job with the USPS is how to find out where the job openings are. Perhaps one of the easiest ways to find a job with the USPS is to look online. First, a warning. Retrieving information for USPS jobs is free. If you come across any websites that provide job listings for a fee, stop there. You should never have to pay to find out about available jobs.

The best place to look for jobs is at www.usps.com. Once there, go to "About USPS & News" at the top of the page. Next, select "Jobs" and, finally, "Apply for Exam." Now, you are ready to search for announcements. You can either enter an announcement number if you already found a job listing, or you can "Continue" the search. At this point, you can enter in the state in which you are looking for a job. Choose your state from the menu and you will see all available job listings with the USPS in that state. Keep in mind that you are looking for jobs that are in or close to the city in which you live and that require Test 473. Once you find that job, click on the announcement number to learn more.

Once you have read through the job listing, you are given the option to apply online to take the exam. However, before you can start the exam application process, you are asked to answer approximately 15 questions. These questions are based on your opinion and experience and you should answer them honestly. (This will be good practice for the Personal Characteristics and Experience Inventory questions.) The answers to the questions will not affect whether or not you are

hired, but if your answers are not positive, it may be an indication that the job does not suit your preferences.

▶ Bulletin Boards

You should always check any job openings advertised at your local post office. It's also important to know that some smaller post offices, especially in rural areas, may keep their recruiting information only at the post office—in other words, it's not found online. You may also want to call your local post office directly to see if it has any openings.

Be sure to check any bulletin boards in local, state, and federal buildings in your area. Even if it's not a post office, you may find USPS job listings in other municipal offices.

▶ State Employment Offices

State employment offices are an excellent source of job listings not only with the USPS, but also with other government organizations. Call or visit your state's employment office regularly to stay aware of any job openings in your area with the USPS.

▶ Postal Job Information Lines

The first thing to note is that most postal districts have what is known as a postal job information line. This is a number you can call to get automated information about current openings and current or upcoming tests. It's usually a simple recording, listing the current job opportunities and providing you with either a phone number or a place to go for an application and further information.

Starting on this page, you'll find a listing of every postal district in the country, including job information lines for the districts that have them. (For postal districts without job information lines, we have provided the phone number to the district personnel office.) Call the job information line in a district in which you are interested in working, listen to the listings, and pay close attention: This is an official listing of where the jobs are. The job information line is a service of the USPS; take advantage of it.

USPS Postal Areas and Postal Districts

What follows is a list of every postal district in the United States, organized alphabetically by state within each postal area. This list is a valuable resource for anyone searching for employment with the USPS, as it provides you with the contact information you need to initiate a job search, especially job information lines.

The postal districts listed there usually encompass several cities, but have their central office in a major city within the district. To find your postal district, look through the list to find the postal area that includes your state (or appropriate portion of your state), and then look for the district in which you fall, usually centered in the nearest major city. For example, if you live in Fort Smith, Arkansas, you'll find the state of Arkansas listed under the Southwest Area; the Arkansas Customer Service District, centered in Little Rock, is the postal district that includes Fort Smith.

Allegheny Area

The Allegheny area includes Delaware (included in the South Jersey Customer Service District), southern New Jersey, Ohio, and Pennsylvania.

South Jersey Customer Service District
Bellmawr, NJ
Job Information Line: 856-933-4262

Akron Customer Service District
Akron, OH
Job Information Line: 330-996-9530

Cincinnati Customer Service District
Cincinnati, OH
Job Information Line: 513-684-5449

Cleveland Customer Service District
Cleveland, OH
Job Information Line: 216-443-4210

Columbus Customer Service District
Columbus, OH
Job Information Line: 614-469-4356

Erie Customer Service District
Erie, PA
Job Information Line: 800-868-6835

Harrisburg Customer Service District
Harrisburg, PA
Job Information Line: 717-257-2191

Philadelphia Customer Service District
Philadelphia, PA
Job Information Line: 215-895-8830

Pittsburgh Customer Service District
Pittsburgh, PA
Job Information Line: 412-359-7516

Great Lakes Area

The Great Lakes area includes Illinois, Indiana, and Michigan.

Central Illinois Customer Service District
Bedford Park, IL
Job Information Line: 708-563-7496

North Illinois Customer Service District
Carol Stream, IL
Job Information Line: 630-260-5200

Chicago Customer Service District
Chicago, IL
Personnel Office: 312-983-8522

Greater Indiana Customer Service District
Indianapolis, IN
Job Information Line: 317-870-8500

Detroit Customer Service District
Detroit, MI
Job Information Line: 313-226-8490

Greater Michigan Customer Service District
Grand Rapids, MI
Personnel Office: 616-776-1426

Royal Oak Customer Service District
Royal Oak, MI
Job Information Line: 248-457-7431

Mid-Atlantic Area

The Mid-Atlantic area includes Kentucky, Maryland, North Carolina, South Carolina, Virginia, Washington, D.C., and West Virginia.

Kentuckiana Customer Service District
Louisville, KY
Job Information Line: 502-454-1625

Baltimore Customer Service District
Baltimore, MD
Job Information Line: 410-347-4320

Mid-Carolinas Customer Service District
Charlotte, NC
Job Information Line: 704-393-4490

Greensboro Customer Service District
Greensboro, NC
Job Information Line: 866-839-7826

Columbia Customer Service District
Casey, SC
Job Information Line: 803-926-6400

Northern Virginia Customer Service District
Merrifield, VA
Job Information Line: 703-698-6561

Richmond Customer Service District
Richmond, VA
Job Information Line: 804-775-6290

Capital Customer Service District
Washington, D.C.
Job Information Line: 301-324-5837

Appalachian Customer Service District
Charleston, WV
Job Information Line: 304-561-1256

Midwest Area

The Midwest area includes Iowa, Kansas (included in the Central Plains Customer Service District in Nebraska), Minnesota, Missouri, Nebraska, North Dakota, South Dakota, and Wisconsin.

Hawkeye Customer Service District
Des Moines, IA
Job Information Line: 515-251-2061

Minneapolis Customer Service District
St. Paul, MN
Job Information Line: 877-293-3364

Mid-America Customer Service District
Kansas City, MO
Job Information Line: 816-374-9346

Gateway Customer Service District
St. Louis, MO
Job Information Line: 314-436-3855

Central Plains Customer Service District
Omaha, NE
Job Information Line: 402-348-2523

Dakotas Customer Service District
Sioux Falls, SD
Job Information Line: 888-725-7854

Milwaukee Customer Service District
Milwaukee, WI
Job Information Line: 414-287-1835

New York Metro Area

The New York metro area includes Long Island, central and northern New Jersey, New York City and Westchester County, and Puerto Rico.

Central New Jersey Customer Service District
Edison, NJ
Job Information Line: 732-819-4334

Northern New Jersey Customer Service District
Newark, NJ
Job Information Line: 866-665-3562

Triboro Customer Service District
Flushing, NY
Job Information Line: 718-529-7000

Long Island Customer Service District
Hauppauge, NY
Job Information Line: 631-582-7530

New York City Customer Service District
New York, NY
Job Information Line: 212-330-3633

Westchester Customer Service District
White Plains, NY
Job Information Line: 914-697-5400

Caribbean Customer Service District
San Juan, PR
Personnel Office: 787-767-3351

Northeast Area

The Northeast area includes Connecticut, Maine, Massachusetts, New Hampshire, upstate New York, Rhode Island, and Vermont (included in the Springfield Customer Service District in Massachusetts).

Connecticut Customer Service District
Hartford, CT
Job Information Line: 860-524-6120

Maine Customer Service District
Portland, ME
Job Information Line: 207-828-8520

Boston Customer Service District
Boston, MA
Job Information Line: 617-654-5569

Middlesex Central Customer Service District
North Reading, MA
Job Information Line: 978-664-7665

Springfield Customer Service District
Springfield, MA
Job Information Line: 1-800-275-8777

New Hampshire Customer Service District
Manchester, NH
Job Information Line: 603-644-4065

Albany Customer Service District
Albany, NY
Job Information Line: 518-452-2445

Western New York Customer Service District
Buffalo, NY
Job Information Line: 716-846-2478

Providence Customer Service District
Providence, RI
Personnel Office: 1-800-275-8777

Pacific Area

The Pacific area includes California and Hawaii.

Los Angeles Customer Service District
Los Angeles, CA
Job Information Line: 323-586-1351

Oakland Customer Service District
Oakland, CA
Job Information Line: 510-251-3040

San Diego Customer Service District
San Diego, CA
Job Information Line: 858-674-0577

San Francisco Customer Service District
San Francisco, CA
Job Information Line: 415-550-5534

San Jose Customer Service District
San Jose, CA
Job Information Line: 408-437-6986

Santa Ana Customer Service District
Santa Ana, CA
Job Information Line: 626-855-6339

Van Nuys Customer Service District
Santa Clarita, CA
Job Information Line: 661-775-7014

Sacramento Customer Service District
West Sacramento, CA
Job Information Line: 916-373-8448

Honolulu Customer Service District
Honolulu, HI
Job Information Line: 1-800-275-8777

Southeast Area

The Southeast area includes Alabama, Florida, Georgia, Mississippi, and Tennessee.

Alabama Customer Service District
Birmingham, AL
Job Information Line: 205-521-0214

North Florida Customer Service District
Jacksonville, FL
Job Information Line: 904-359-2737

Central Florida Customer Service District
Mid Florida, FL
Job Information Line: 407-444-2029

South Florida Customer Service District
Pembroke Pines, FL
Job Information Line: 305-470-0412

Sun Coast Customer Service District
Tampa, FL
Job Information Line: 813-877-0381

Atlanta Customer Service District
Atlanta, GA
Job Information Line: 770-717-3470

South Georgia Customer Service District
Macon, GA
Job Information Line: 478-752-8465

Mississippi Customer Service District
Jackson, MS
Job Information Line: 601-351-7099

Tennessee Customer Service District
Nashville, TN
Job Information Line: 615-885-9190

Southwest Area

The Southwest area includes Arkansas, Louisiana, Oklahoma, and Texas.

Arkansas Customer Service District
Little Rock, AR
Job Information Line: 501-945-6665

New Orleans Customer Service District
New Orleans, LA
Job Information Line: 888-421-4887

Oklahoma Customer Service District
Oklahoma City, OK
Job Information Line: 1-800-275-8777

Dallas Customer Service District
Coppell, TX
Job Information Line: 214-760-4531

Fort Worth Customer Service District
Fort Worth, TX
Job Information Line: 817-317-3366

Houston Customer Service District
Houston, TX
Job Information Line: 713-226-3872

San Antonio Customer Service District
San Antonio, TX
Personnel Office: 210-368-8400

Western Area

The Western area includes Alaska, Arizona, Colorado, Montana, New Mexico, Nevada, Oregon, Utah, Washington, and Wyoming (included in the Denver Customer Service District in Colorado).

Anchorage Customer Service District
Anchorage, AK
Job Information Line: 907-564-2964

Phoenix Customer Service District
Phoenix, AZ
Job Information Line: 602-223-3624

Denver Customer Service District
Denver, CO
Job Information Line: 877-482-3238

Billings Customer Service District
Billings, MT
Job Information Line: 406-657-5763

Albuquerque Customer Service District
Albuquerque, NM
Job Information Line: 505-346-8780

Las Vegas Customer Service District
Las Vegas, NV
Job Information Line: 702-361-9564

Here is a brief outline of the process of applying for and taking Test 473:

1. The USPS announces Test 473 openings to fill a position of city carrier, mail processing clerk, mail handler, or sales, services, and distribution associate.
2. Apply for Test 473 online* or by calling the toll-free number found on the job announcement.
3. You are sent information on the exam date, time, and location.
4. You take Test 473.
5. The National Test Center Administration scores your test.
6. If you do not pass, you will be informed that you will not be considered for employment with the USPS. If you do pass, your name is placed on a register. Keep reading to learn more about scoring on Test 473 and the importance of the register.

---

* When applying for Test 473 online, applicants are required to answer approximately 15 questions about their interests and preferences relating to work. Although the answers to these questions do not affect selection, they are intended to determine an applicant's genuine interest in the position.

Portland Customer Service District
Portland, OR
Job Information Line: 503-294-2270

Salt Lake City Customer Service District
Salt Lake City, UT
Job Information Line: 801-974-2209

Seattle Customer Service District
Seattle, WA
Job Information Line: 206-442-6240

Spokane Customer Service District
Spokane, WA
Job Information Line: 509-626-6896

▶ Be Active

If you want a job, you have to be an active seeker. Make it a point to check local bulletin boards, go online, or visit state employment offices regularly. Remember, you may have just a couple of days' notice for an application period, and there may not be another one in the same area for several years.

▶ Test 473

The Postal Worker Exam, Test 473, is a national, standardized test given by the USPS to evaluate the skill levels of applicants for the following entry-level positions:

- City carrier
- Mail processing clerk
- Mail handler
- Sales, services, and distribution associate

CHAPTER

2 ▶ Test 473 Content

CHAPTER SUMMARY

Now that you have a good idea of what it's like to work for the USPS, what the hiring process is, and how Test 473 is administered, you are probably wondering what types of questions are actually on the exam. This chapter describes the content of Test 473. And of course, you need to know more about how the test is scored and how to avoid common errors when taking the test.

Every year, hundreds of thousands of people apply for a job with the USPS. Only a small percentage of them is hired. You've taken the first step in gaining a competitive advantage for yourself by using this book. If you haven't yet studied the specifics of Test 473, here's a review of the test's content, including info on how to get the test score you need for the job you want.

Test 473 Content Breakdown

The test, created in 2004, streamlines the hiring process for the aforementioned entry-level positions.

Test 473 assesses attention to detail, accuracy, memory, and your interest in this type of work. It doesn't test knowledge of facts. The test is broken into four parts (A, B, C, and D), with Part C having two sections:

- **Part A—Address Checking** (60 questions, 11 minutes)
  Task: Determine if two lists of addresses are the same. This part requires speed and accuracy.
- **Part B—Forms Completion** (30 questions, 15 minutes)
  Task: Identify how a form is correctly completed.

- **Part C, Section 1—Coding** (36 questions, 6 minutes)
  Task: Using a guide, identify the route or code to which a certain address is assigned.
- **Part C, Section 2—Memory** (36 questions, 7 minutes)
  Task: From memory, identify the route to which a certain address belongs.
- **Part D—Personal Characteristics and Experience Inventory** (236 questions, 90 minutes)
  Task: Answer the questions as honestly and accurately as possible, to determine how well you will fit in the USPS culture.

Test 473 Format

All of the questions on Test 473 are multiple choice, and every question has four answer choices: **a, b, c**, and **d**. To learn more about the format of each part of the test, read the sections that follow or turn to the specific chapter that covers that part in detail.

You must work on one part of the test at a time. You cannot go forward to another part if you finish early, nor go back to a previous part.

Test 473 Scoring

When you take Test 473, your tests are sent to the National Test Administration Center to be scored. Here is roughly how this occurs with each part of your exam:

- For **Part A**, you receive one point for every correct answer. You receive no points for questions you do not answer. For each question that you get wrong, $\frac{1}{3}$ of a point will be subtracted from the points you do have. For example, let's say you answer 50 questions, 41 of them correctly. You have 41 points for correct answers, but you were wrong on 9 questions; 9 times $\frac{1}{3}$ (because it's $\frac{1}{3}$ of every point) = 3. Now you subtract 3 from 41, and you earned 38 points on Part A. The USPS suggests that you do not guess at answers in this

part unless you can eliminate some answer choices.

- For **Part B**, you receive one point for every correct answer. You receive no points for questions you do not answer. However, unlike Part A, there is no penalty for incorrect answers. So, as many questions as you get right is your score.
- Although **Part C** is given in two sections, both are scored the same. You receive one point for every correct answer and no points for questions you do not answer. Like Part A, $\frac{1}{3}$ of a point will be deducted for every incorrect answer you give.
- **Part D** is unlike any other part of Test 473. In this section—which happens to be the longest—there are no correct or incorrect answers. The questions are meant to reflect your feelings, opinions, and preferences about work. The goal here is to be as honest as possible. The USPS has not released information about how this section is "scored," but the honesty and accuracy of your answers will affect your overall score. To learn more about this unusual part of the test, see Chapter 8.

Here's how your score on each part is determined. The "raw" scores you receive are added up. By using a formula created and used exclusively by the USPS, a raw score is converted to a basic rating. The basic rating is a score between 1 and 100. A basic rating of 70 is required to pass the test and continue in the hiring process.

Veteran's Preference

Veterans of the U.S. military receive special privileges and preferences in scoring and selection. Some family members of disabled or deceased veterans may also fall into this category. Veterans are granted an additional five or ten points on Test 473, making for a best possible score of 110. To learn more about Veteran's Preference, contact your local post office's personnel department.

Test 473 Scores and the Register

The names of all applicants who score a basic rating of 70 or above are placed on a register, a list used by the USPS to rank all eligible applicants in order of score, from highest to lowest. Applicants are hired from the register, starting with those who are highest on the register. Although a basic rating of 70 is considered passing, it is unlikely to get you hired. Due to the intense competition for postal jobs, you will want to aim for the highest score you can, ideally in the high eighties or nineties.

Registers can remain valid for two years and may be extended beyond that depending on hiring needs and the availability of applicants on other registers. When local postal facilities need to fill positions, they turn to their registers, starting from the top, and continue the screening process by selecting several names from the list.

When offering an exam, a postal facility usually has already determined that it has a need for new employees, so the top names are selected immediately.

This is not always the case, however. Names can be selected from a register a year or more after the test has been given, for as long as the register is valid. When you take an exam, the first round of hiring will probably take place as soon as the tests are scored, and hopefully your name will be among those selected. If not, your name will remain on the register, and the next time positions open up, the postal facility or district that tested you will turn to that register for its next group of applicants.

It's very important to remember that names on the register are ranked by score. When a postal facility takes names from a register, it starts at the top and moves down through the list. Also, keep in mind that the names of veterans with compensable disabilities who passed the exam are placed on top of the entire register, before all other applicants. The bottom line is, it's extremely important to score as high as possible; even one point can make a difference.

Part A—Address Checking Content and Format

Part A—Address Checking may sound self explanatory, but to do your best on this section, you must know what is expected of you. First, there are 60 multiple-choice questions and 11 minutes in which you are required to answer them. However, it's important to note that you may not be able to answer every question. This part is testing your speed and accuracy, so don't just randomly fill in bubbles as time is running out. This is especially important because for every incorrect answer, $\frac{1}{3}$ of a point will be deducted from your score. Instead, you should work quickly without sacrificing accuracy. Here is a sample question:

	CORRECT LIST		LIST TO BE CHECKED	
QUESTION	ADDRESS	ZIP CODE	ADDRESS	ZIP CODE
1.	1611 Dennis Dr		1611 Ennis Dr	
	Jonesville, LA	71343-9643	Jonesville, LA	71343-9643

a. No errors
b. Address only
c. ZIP code only
d. Both

To answer each question, you have to review and compare the information in the "List to Be Checked" with the information in the "Correct List." Then you have to decide if there are no errors (meaning both addresses and ZIP codes are identical), an error in the address column only, an error in the ZIP code column only, or if there are errors in both the address and ZIP code columns.

To learn more about this section and to review the strategies that will help you score as many points as possible, don't miss Chapter 5, Address Checking Review.

Test 473 includes four parts—one part has two sections—with the following breakdown:

SECTION NAME	NUMBER OF QUESTIONS	TIME	SCORING
Part A—Address Checking	60	11 minutes	Guessing penalty of $\frac{1}{3}$ off each incorrect answer
Part B—Forms Completion	30	15 minutes	No guessing penalty
Part C, Section 1—Coding	36	6 minutes	Guessing penalty of $\frac{1}{3}$ off each incorrect answer
Part C, Section 2—Memory	36	7 minutes	Guessing penalty of $\frac{1}{3}$ off each incorrect answer
Part D—Personal Characteristics and Experience Inventory	236	90 minutes	No specific scoring information available.
TOTAL	398 questions	129 minutes	A passing score is a "basic rating" score between 70–100. There is no specific information given by the USPS about how scores are converted.

Part B—Forms Completion Content and Format

Forms Completion questions in Part B of Test 473 might also seem clear-cut. In fact, they are. However, that doesn't mean that they are simple. You still have to work quickly because you must answer 30 multiple-choice questions in only 15 minutes. Although you have only 30 seconds to answer each question, you are expected to answer all of the questions. But remember, no points are deducted for incorrect answers, so answer every question even if you are guessing randomly as time is running out.

All questions are preceded by a sample blank form similar to those used by the USPS (see the following). After this form are questions, such as this one:

1. Which of the following is an appropriate entry for box 3A?
   a. $67.00
   b. 6/7/2009
   c. Tucson
   d. Massachusetts

To answer these questions, you have to review the form and decide which choice is correct. In this case, the answer is **b**; box 3A requires a date. If you want to learn more about how to improve your score on this part of Test 473, turn to Chapter 6, Forms Completion Review.

Sample Form

1. Last Name	
1A. First Name	
2. Address	
2A. City	
2B. State	2C. ZIP Code
3. Signature	
3A. Date	4. Postmark

Part C—Coding and Memory Content and Format

Part C is actually made up of two sections. Section 1 is Coding and Section 2 is Memory. Each section has 36 multiple-choice questions for a total of 72 questions. The timing does vary by section. For example, in the Coding section, you have six minutes to answer all the questions. For the Memory section, you will have three minutes for memorization and seven minutes to answer the questions. These two sections have the shortest testing times, so you are not expected to answer every question. However, because $\frac{1}{3}$ of a point is deducted for incorrect answers, you should be careful when answering and you should not guess randomly if time is running out.

The questions in both sections are preceded by a "Coding Guide" similar to the following one.

CODING GUIDE	
ADDRESS RANGE	**DELIVERY ROUTE**
50–300 Up Ave 1–20 Down Street	A
700–1550 Here Blvd 600–1200 Somewhere Lane 10–80 N There Street	B
81–120 N There Street 1700–2200 Here Blvd 1201–1700 Somewhere Lane	C
All mail that doesn't belong in one of the address ranges listed here.	D

Each question consists of an address that belongs in one of the three delivery routes: A, B, or C. If the given address doesn't belong in one of those routes, the answer is D. Here is a sample question:

1. 1754 Here Blvd
   a. Delivery Route A
   b. Delivery Route B
   c. Delivery Route C
   d. Delivery Route D

In this case, the answer is **c**; 1754 falls in the range of 1700–2200 Here Blvd, so it belongs in delivery route C.

The difference between Coding questions and Memory questions is this: While answering Coding questions, you are able to refer back to the Coding Guide as often as needed. In the Memory section, the exact same Coding Guide is given, but you are only given three minutes to memorize it. You are not able to take notes during the study period, and while answering the seven-minute Memory section, you are not able to refer back to the Coding Guide.

To score your best, read and use the strategies offered in Chapter 7, Coding and Memory Review.

Part D—Personal Characteristics and Experience Inventory Content and Format

Part D is unlike any other part of Test 473. In fact, it's different from any test, really. Why? Well, the 236 multiple-choice questions, which you must answer in 90 minutes, do not have correct or incorrect answers. (In Chapter 8, you will find an abbreviated version of the test—60 questions—and it should take you no more than 20 minutes to complete it.) The section consists of three question types: Agree/Disagree, Very Often/Rarely or Never, and Experience. Each question type is intended to gauge your suitability for a job with the USPS, and the scoring instructions following our abbreviated version should give you an idea of how tests of this nature are generally analyzed and

scored. There's really only one way to answer these questions: HONESTLY. To learn more about this unique section of Test 473, read Chapter 8, Personal Characteristics and Experience Inventory Review and Questions.

▶ Additional Review

You've learned a lot of helpful information about finding a job with the USPS. However, you are probably feeling as though you have a lot more to learn in order to do your best on test day. To learn strategies to improve your score on Test 473, turn to Chapters 5–8.

Ten Ways to Avoid Errors

1. Work quickly.
2. Work carefully.
3. Be aware of exactly which question and section you are working on.
4. Stay focused only on what you are doing.
5. Take time to study each form in Part B.
6. Answer easier items first.
7. Return to more difficult items later, if time permits.
8. Guess only if you can eliminate at least one choice as incorrect.
9. Fully use the time you have to memorize the codes.
10. Read statements in Part D carefully before answering.

3 ▶ The LearningExpress Test Preparation System

CHAPTER SUMMARY

Test 473, the Postal Worker Exam, demands a lot of preparation if you want to be one of the few who achieve a top score and reach the next stage in the hiring process. The LearningExpress Test Preparation System, developed exclusively for LearningExpress by leading test experts, gives you the discipline and attitude you need to get the job you want.

Your future career as a postal worker depends on your getting a high score, but there are all sorts of pitfalls that can keep you from doing your best on this all-important exam. Here are some steps to take to improve your chance of success.

- Be familiar with the format of this exam.
- Conquer test anxiety.
- Set aside enough time to prepare and study.
- Begin to prepare well in advance of your test date.
- Know vital test-taking skills: how to pace yourself through the exam, how to use the process of elimination, and when to guess.
- Be in tip-top mental and physical shape.
- Arrive on time at the test site, eat a filling meal, and wear comfortable, temperature-appropriate clothes.

What's the common denominator in all these test-taking strategies? One word: control. Who's in control, you or the exam?

The LearningExpress Test Preparation System puts you in control. In just nine easy-to-follow steps, you will learn everything you need to know to make sure that you are in charge of your preparation and your performance on the exam. Other test takers may let the test get the better of them; other test takers may be unprepared or out of shape, but not you. You will have taken all the steps you need to take to get a high score on Test 473.

Here's how the LearningExpress Test Preparation System works: Nine easy steps lead you through everything you need to know and do to get ready to master your exam. Each of the steps listed here includes reading about the step and about one or more activities. It's important that you do the activities along with the reading, or you won't be getting the full benefit of the system. Each step tells you approximately how much time that step will take you to complete.

Step 1. Get Information	30 minutes
Step 2. Conquer Test Anxiety	20 minutes
Step 3. Make a Plan	50 minutes
Step 4. Learn to Manage Your Time	10 minutes
Step 5. Learn to Use the Process of Elimination	20 minutes
Step 6. Know When to Guess	20 minutes
Step 7. Reach Your Peak Performance Zone	10 minutes
Step 8. Get Your Act Together	10 minutes
Step 9. Do It!	10 minutes
Total	3 hours

We estimate that working through the entire system will take you approximately three hours, although it's perfectly fine if you work faster or slower than we estimated. If you can take a whole afternoon or evening, you can work through the whole Learning-Express Test Preparation System in one sitting. Otherwise, you can break it up, and do just one or two steps a day for the next several days. It's up to you—remember, you are in control.

▶ Step 1: Get Information

Time to complete: 30 minutes
Activities: Read Chapter 2, Test 473 Content

The first step in the LearningExpress Test Preparation System is finding out everything you can about the Test 473. Once you have your information, the next steps in the LearningExpress Test Preparation System will show you what to do about it.

Part A: Straight Talk about Test 473

Why do you have to take this exam, anyway? The fact is that a lot people want a secure job with the USPS, far more than can ever be hired—far more, in fact, than the USPS can even afford to process in a conventional application-resume-interview process. The USPS needs a way to reduce dramatically the number of applicants they have to consider. That's where the exam comes in.

Test 473 is a screening device. It enables the USPS to rank candidates according to their exam scores and then to pull only from the top of that list to get applicants to go through the rest of the hiring process. Since Test 473 assesses job-related skills—abilities you have to have to be a good postal worker—there's a general correlation between how well a person does on the test and how good a postal employee that person will be. So the USPS, like most government agencies, uses an exam simply to cut the number of applicants it accepts into the hiring process.

Part B: What's on the Test

Test 473 consists of four parts (one part has two sections), each of which is timed separately.

You will learn more about each part of the exam in the review chapters (Chapters 5–8).

PART	NUMBER OF QUESTIONS	TIME
Part A—Address Checking	60	11 minutes
Part B—Forms Completion	30	15 minutes
Part C, Section 1—Coding	36	6 minutes
Part C, Section 2—Memory	36	7 minutes
Part D—Personal Characteristics and Experience Inventory	236	90 minutes
TOTAL	398 questions	Approximately 130 minutes

▶ Step 2: Conquer Test Anxiety

Time to complete: 20 minutes
Activity: Take the Test Stress Test

Having complete information about the exam is the first step in getting control of the exam. Next, you have to overcome one of the biggest obstacles to test success: test anxiety. Test anxiety can not only impair your performance on the exam itself; it can even keep you from preparing. In Step 2, you will learn stress management techniques that will help you succeed on Test 473. Learn these strategies now, and practice them as you work through the exams in this book so they will be second nature to you by exam day.

Combating Test Anxiety

The first thing you need to know is that a little test anxiety is a good thing. Everyone gets nervous before a big exam—and if that nervousness motivates you to prepare thoroughly, so much the better. Some test stress can give you a little extra edge—just the kind of edge you need to do well.

On page 28 is the Test Stress Test. Stop here and answer the questions on that page to find out whether your level of test anxiety is something you should worry about.

You need to worry about test anxiety only if it is extreme enough to impair your performance. The following questionnaire will provide a diagnosis of your level of test anxiety. In the blank before each statement, write the number that most accurately describes your experience.

0 = Never   1 = Once or twice   2 = Sometimes   3 = Often

_____ I have gotten so nervous before an exam that I simply put down the books and didn't study for it.

_____ I have experienced disabling physical symptoms such as vomiting and severe headaches because I was nervous about an exam.

_____ I have simply not shown up for an exam because I was scared to take it.

_____ I have experienced dizziness and disorientation while taking an exam.

_____ I have had trouble filling in the little circles because my hands were shaking too much.

_____ I have failed an exam because I was too nervous to complete it.

_____ **Total: Add up the numbers in the blanks above.**

Your Test Stress Score

Here are the steps you should take, depending on your score. If you scored:

- **Below 3,** your level of test anxiety is nothing to worry about; it's probably just enough to give you that little extra edge.

- **Between 3 and 6,** your test anxiety may be enough to impair your performance, and you should practice the stress management techniques listed in this section to try to bring your test anxiety down to manageable levels.

- **Above 6,** your level of test anxiety is a concern. In addition to practicing the stress management techniques listed in this section, you may want to seek additional help. Call your local community college and ask for the academic counselor. Tell the academic counselor that you have a level of test anxiety that sometimes keeps you from being able to take an exam. He or she may be willing to help you or may suggest someone else you should talk to.

Stress Management before the Test

If you feel your level of anxiety getting the best of you in the weeks before the test, here is what you need to do to bring the level down again:

- **Get prepared.** There's nothing like knowing what to expect and being prepared for it to put you in control of test anxiety. That's why you're reading this book. Use it faithfully, and remind yourself that you're better prepared than most of the people taking the test.

- **Practice self-confidence.** A positive attitude is a great way to combat test anxiety. This is no time to be humble or shy. Stand in front of the mirror and say to your reflection, "I'm prepared. I'm full of self-confidence. I'm going to ace this test. I know I can do it." Say it into a tape recorder and play it back once a day. If you hear it often enough, you will believe it.

- **Fight negative messages.** Every time someone starts telling you how hard the exam is or how it's almost impossible to get a high score, start telling them your self-confidence messages. If the someone with the negative messages is you, telling yourself you don't do well on exams, you just can't do this—don't listen. Turn on your tape recorder and listen to your self-confidence messages.
- **Visualize.** Imagine yourself walking your route as a postal carrier or operating a sorting machine. Think of yourself coming home with your first paycheck as a USPS employee and taking your family or friends out to celebrate. Visualizing success can help make it happen—and it reminds you of why you're going through all this work in preparing for the exam.
- **Exercise.** Physical activity helps calm your body down and focus your mind. Besides, being in good physical shape can actually help you do well on the exam. Go for a run, lift weights, go swimming—and do it regularly.

Stress Management on Test Day

You can bring down your level of test anxiety on test day. They will work best if you practice them in the weeks before the test, so you know which ones work best for you.

- **Deep breathing.** Take a deep breath while you count to five. Hold it for a count of one, and then let it out as you count to five. Repeat several times.
- **Move your body.** Try rolling your head in a circle. Rotate your shoulders. Shake your hands from the wrist. Many people find these movements very relaxing.
- **Visualize again.** Think of the place where you are most relaxed: lying on the beach in the sun, walking through the park—wherever you feel at peace. Now, close your eyes and imagine you're actually there. If you practice in advance, you will find that you need only a few seconds of this exercise

to experience a significant increase in your sense of well-being.

When anxiety threatens to overwhelm you right there during the exam, there are still things you can do to manage the stress level:

- **Repeat your self-confidence messages.** You should have them memorized by now. Say them silently to yourself, and believe them.
- **Visualize one more time.** This time, visualize yourself moving smoothly and quickly through the test answering every question right. Like most visualization techniques, this one works best if you have practiced it ahead of time.
- **Take a mental break.** Everyone loses concentration once in a while during a long test. It's normal, so you shouldn't worry about it. Instead, accept what has happened. Say to yourself, "Hey, I lost it there for a minute. My brain is taking a break." Put down your pencil, close your eyes, and do some deep breathing for a few seconds. Then you're ready to go back to work.

Try these techniques ahead of time, and see if they work for you.

▶ Step 3: Make a Plan

Time to complete: 50 minutes
Activity: Construct a study plan

Maybe the most important thing you can do to get control of yourself and your exam is to make a study plan. Too many people fail to prepare simply because they fail to plan. Spending hours on the day before the exam poring over sample test questions not only raises your level of test anxiety, but is also simply no substitute for careful preparation and practice over time.

Don't fall into the cram trap. Take control of your preparation time by mapping out a study schedule.

What follows are two sample schedules, each based on the amount of time you have before Test 473. If you're the kind of person who needs deadlines and assignments to motivate you for a project, here they are. If you're the kind of person who doesn't like to follow other people's plans, you can use the suggested schedules here to construct your own.

Even more important than making a plan is making a commitment. You can't improve your memory, speed, and accuracy overnight. You have to set aside some time every day for study and practice. Try for at least 20 minutes a day. Twenty minutes daily will do you much more good than two hours on Saturday.

If you have months before the exam, you're lucky. Don't put off your study until the week before the exam. Start now. A few minutes a day, with half an hour or more on weekends, can make a big difference in your score—and in your chances of getting the job!

Schedule A: One month (or more) before the exam

If you have at least one month before the exam, you have enough time for some concentrated study that will help you improve your score.

DAY	ACTIVITY
Days 1–2	Review the materials in Chapters 1 and 2. Make sure you understand the job descriptions and are familiar with the form and content of Test 473.
Day 3	Read through the LearningExpress Test Preparation System (Chapter 3).
Day 4	Take the first practice test in Chapter 4.
Day 5	Score the first practice test. Use the information at the end of Chapter 4 to calculate your raw score. Make note of your strengths and weaknesses.
Days 6–9	Review the section that gave you the most trouble in the first practice test. Use the study material in Chapters 5–7.
Day 10	Read through the information in Chapter 8 about the Personal Characteristics and Experience Inventory section of the test.
Day 11	Review another section of the first practice test that gave you trouble. Use the study material in Chapters 5–7.
Days 12–13	Take the second practice test in Chapter 9.
Day 14	Score the second practice test. Make note of any areas that still need improvement.
Day 15	To improve your score, review the study material in Chapters 5–7.
Days 16–18	Go back and review the material in Chapter 8 regarding the Personal Characteristics and Experience Inventory section of the test.
Days 19–20	Take the third practice test in Chapter 10.
Day 21	Score the third practice test and make note of any weaknesses.
Days 22–24	Review any areas that are still giving you trouble. Use the study material in Chapters 5–7.

DAY	ACTIVITY
Days 25–26	Take the final practice test in Chapter 11.
Day 27	Score the final practice test and see how much you have improved.
Days 28–29	Review Chapters 5–8 once again to make sure there isn't any strategy or information you might have missed.
Day before the exam	Relax. Do something unrelated to the exam. Eat a good meal and go to bed at your usual time.

Schedule B: Ten days to the exam

If you have ten days or fewer before the exam, you really have your work cut out for you. Carve an hour out of your day, every day, for study. This schedule assumes you have just ten days to prepare; if you have more or less time, you will have to expand or compress the schedule accordingly.

DAY	ACTIVITY
Day 1	Take the first practice test in Chapter 4. Score the test and use the information at the end of Chapter 4 to calculate your raw score. Make note of your strengths and weaknesses.
Day 2	Review the section that gave you the most trouble in the first practice. Use the study material in Chapters 5–7.
Day 3	Read through the information in Chapter 8 about the Personal Characteristics and Experience Inventory section of the test, and spend time answering the questions as honestly as you can.
Day 4	Take the second practice test in Chapter 9. Score the test and use the information at the end of Chapter 9 to calculate your raw score. Make note of your strengths and weaknesses.
Day 5	To improve your score, review the study material in Chapters 5–7.
Day 6	Take the third practice test in Chapter 10. Score the third practice test and make note of any weaknesses.
Day 7	Review any areas that are still giving you trouble. Use the study material in Chapters 5–7.
Day 8	Take the final practice test in Chapter 11. Score the final practice test and see how much you have improved.
Day 9	Review Chapters 5–8 once again to make sure there isn't any strategy or information you might have missed.
Day before the exam	Relax. Do something unrelated to the exam. Eat a good meal and go to bed at your usual time.

► Step 4: Learn to Manage Your Time

Time to complete: 10 minutes to read, many hours to perfect

Activities: Practice these strategies as you take the practice tests in this book

Steps 4, 5, and 6 of the LearningExpress Test Preparation System put you in charge of your exam by showing you test-taking strategies that work. Practice these strategies as you take the sample tests in this book, and then you'll be ready to use them on test day.

First, you will take control of your time on the exam. Each of the sections of Test 473 is timed separately, and none of them allows you a whole lot of time. Thus, you should use your time wisely to avoid making errors and to answer as many questions as you can. The chapters in this book on each part of the exam offer you time-management strategies for that section. Here are some general tips for the whole exam.

- **Listen carefully to directions.** By the time you get to the exam, you should know the directions for all four parts of the test, but listen just in case something has changed.
- **Keep moving.** You don't have time to waste on one question. If you don't know the answer, skip the question and move on.
- **Keep track of your place on the answer sheet.** If you skip a question, make sure you skip on the answer sheet, too. Check yourself every five to ten questions to make sure the question number and the answer sheet number are still the same.
- **Work quickly AND accurately.** Although you should keep moving, rushing through and making careless errors won't help. Try to keep calm and work methodically and quickly.

► Step 5: Learn to Use the Process of Elimination

Time to complete: 20 minutes

Activity: Use the process of elimination on the practice questions in this section

Although this skill doesn't directly apply to all parts of Test 473, it is a good skill to have in life and at work. Standard test-taking wisdom says that you should always read all the answer choices before choosing your answer and eliminate wrong answer choices to help you find the right answer. Of course, you don't actually have to read the answer choices on Parts A and C of the exam, because the answer choices are always the same.

Here is how the process of elimination works on Part C—Coding and Memory.

Process of Elimination on Part C—Coding and Memory

How well you can use the process of elimination on Part C—Coding and Memory, depends on how well you managed to use and memorize the Coding Guide in the first place. If you're confident about the content of all the boxes, you're all set—you won't have to use the process of elimination. But suppose you ran out of time during the memorization segment and were only able to get the contents of Boxes A and B down cold; you're a little fuzzy on Box C. (Or maybe you had all of them down cold a few minutes ago, but now you're starting to doubt whether you've confused some of the address elements in those last boxes.)

So, then let's say that question 5 is 1751 Mayberry Lane. You think it through and find that 1751 Mayberry Lane isn't among the ranges you memorized for Boxes A or B. But you don't know whether it's in Box C or perhaps, Box D, where all address ranges not in the previous boxes are included. You've just used the process of elimination. You know that two of the possible answers are wrong, and only two have the possibility of being right. As you will see when you read

Step 6 on guessing, if you can eliminate even one wrong answer choice, you should go ahead and mark one of the possible answers.

That's how process of elimination works. It's your tool for the next step, which is knowing when to guess.

▶ Step 6: Know When to Guess

Time to complete: 20 minutes
Activity: Complete worksheet on Your Guessing Ability

Armed with the process of elimination, you're ready to take control of one of the big questions in test taking: Should I guess? The first and main answer is Yes. Unless parts of the exam have a so-called guessing penalty, which Test 473 does, you have nothing to lose from guessing. The more complicated answer depends both on the exam and on you—your personality and your "guessing intuition."

Guessing and Test 473

Part A and both sections of Part C on Test 473 have a guessing penalty, while Parts B and D have no such penalty. On Parts A and C, you will lose $\frac{1}{3}$ point for every incorrect answer.

How the "Guessing Penalty" Works

A "guessing penalty" really only works against random guessing—filling in the little circles with no relation to the answers. If you can eliminate one or more answer choices, you're better off taking a guess than leaving the answer blank, even on the sections that have a penalty.

In short, if you're running out of time on Part A or either section of Part C, you should not use your remaining seconds to fill in the rest of the bubbles on your answer sheet. Take those few seconds to try to answer one more question correctly.

Sections That Don't Have a Guessing Penalty

On Part B, it's always safe to guess—especially if you've been able to eliminate one or more wrong answer choices. It's even safe to mark answers at random if you find that you are running out of time and haven't gotten to all the questions. Those wrong answers can't count against you—and you just might get one or two right, purely by chance.

On Part D, there is no right or wrong answer. Remember that on those questions, your goal is to answer honestly.

Guessing and You

The other factor in deciding whether or not to guess, besides the exam, is you. There are two things you need to know about yourself before you go into the exam:

- Are you a risk-taker?
- Are you a good guesser?

These questions matter most on the sections that have guessing penalties. Even if you're a play-it-safe person with lousy intuition, guessing on other sections is perfectly safe. Overcome your anxieties, and go ahead and mark an answer.

But when you know your guess could count against you when you're wrong, your own personal risk-taking temperament and guessing skills do factor in. Complete the worksheet titled Your Guessing Ability on page 34 to get an idea of how good your intuition is.

Following are ten really hard questions. You're not supposed to know the answers. Rather, this is an assessment of your ability to guess when you don't have a clue. Read each question carefully, just as if you did expect to answer it. If you have any knowledge at all of the subject of the question, use that knowledge to help you eliminate wrong answer choices. Use this answer grid to fill in your answers to the questions.

1. (a) (b) (c) (d)   **5.** (a) (b) (c) (d)   **9.** (a) (b) (c) (d)
2. (a) (b) (c) (d)   **6.** (a) (b) (c) (d)   **10.** (a) (b) (c) (d)
3. (a) (b) (c) (d)   **7.** (a) (b) (c) (d)
4. (a) (b) (c) (d)   **8.** (a) (b) (c) (d)

1. The balboa is the monetary unit of
   a. Sweden
   b. Thailand
   c. Panama
   d. Togo

2. The Ross Dependency in Antarctica is administered by
   a. Chile
   b. Argentina
   c. Iceland
   d. New Zealand

3. In England, Guy Fawkes Day is observed on
   a. November 5
   b. October 12
   c. February 22
   d. July 4

4. The first U.S. Secretary of the Treasury was
   a. Thomas Jefferson
   b. Oliver Wolcott
   c. Alexander Hamilton
   d. John Adams

5. American author Willa Cather was born in
   a. 1925
   b. 1801
   c. 1873
   d. 1950

6. Which of the following was NOT written by Octavio Paz?
   a. *The Labyrinth of Solitude*
   b. *Toward the Splendid City*
   c. *They Shall Not Pass!*
   d. *The Sun Shone*

7. Which of the following is the formula for determining the momentum of an object?
   a. $p = mv$
   b. $F = ma$
   c. $P = IV$
   d. $E = mc^2$

8. In 1890, the center of the U.S. population was east of
   a. Columbus, IN
   b. Steelville, MO
   c. Parkersburg, WV
   d. Baltimore, MD

9. Because of the expansion of the universe, the stars and other celestial bodies are all moving away from one another. This phenomenon is known as
   a. Newton's first law.
   b. the Big Bang.
   c. gravitational collapse.
   d. Hubble flow.

10. Which of these entertainers was originally named Caryn Johnson?
   a. Erykah Badu
   b. Cher
   c. Billie Holiday
   d. Whoopi Goldberg

Answers

Check your answers against the correct answers below.

   1. c.
   2. d.
   3. a.
   4. c.
   5. c.
   6. b.
   7. a.
   8. a.
   9. d.
   10. d.

How Did You Do?

You may have known the answer to one or two questions. Knowing about a particular subject may have made your guesses more successful because you were able to use the process of elimination. Maybe you didn't know who the first Secretary of the Treasury was (question 4), but you knew that John Adams was the first vice president. In that case, you would have eliminated answer **d** and therefore improved your odds of guessing right from one in four to one in three.

According to probability, you should get $2\frac{1}{2}$ answers correct, so getting either two or three right would be average. If you got four or more right, you may be a really terrific guesser. If you got one or none right, you may be a really bad guesser.

Keep in mind, though, that this is only a small sample. You should continue to keep track of your guessing ability as you work through the sample questions in this book. Circle the numbers of questions you guess on as you make your guess; or, if you don't have time while you take the practice tests, go back afterward and try to remember which questions you guessed at.

▶ Step 7: Reach Your Peak Performance Zone

Time to complete: 10 minutes to read, weeks to complete!
Activity: Complete the Physical Preparation Checklist

To get ready for a challenge like a big exam, you have to take control of your physical, as well as your mental, state. Exercise, proper diet, and rest will ensure that your body works with your mind, rather than against it, on test day as well as during your preparation.

Exercise

If you don't already have a regular exercise program, the time during which you're preparing for an exam is actually an excellent time to start one. And if you're already keeping fit—or trying to get that way—don't let the pressure of preparing for an exam fool you into quitting now. Exercise helps reduce stress by pumping wonderful good-feeling hormones called endorphins into your system. It also increases the oxygen supply throughout your body, including your brain, so you will be at peak performance on test day.

A half hour of vigorous activity—enough to break a sweat—every day should be your aim. If you're really pressed for time, every other day is okay. Choose an activity you like and get out there and do it. Jogging with a friend always makes the time go faster, or take a radio.

But don't overdo. You don't want to exhaust yourself. Moderation is the key.

Diet

First, cut out the junk and nicotine. Go easy on caffeine and eliminate alcohol from your system for at least two weeks before the exam.

What your body needs for peak performance is simply a balanced diet. Eat plenty of fruits and vegetables, along with protein and carbohydrates. Foods that are high in lecithin (an amino acid), such as fish and beans, are especially good "brain foods."

The night before the exam, you might "carbo-load" the way athletes do before a contest. Eat a big plate of spaghetti, rice and beans, or whatever your favorite carbohydrate is.

Rest

You probably know how much sleep you need every night to be at your best, even if you don't always get it. Make sure you do get that much sleep, though, for at least a week before the exam. Moderation is important here, too. Extra sleep will just make you groggy.

If you're not a morning person and your exam will be given in the morning, you should reset your internal clock so that your body doesn't think you're taking an exam at 3 A.M. You have to start this process well before the exam. The way it works is to get up half an hour earlier each morning, and then go to bed half an hour earlier that night. Don't try it the other way around; you will just toss and turn if you go to bed early

without having gotten up early. The next morning, get up another half an hour earlier, and so on. How long you will have to do this depends on how late you're used to getting up.

▶ Step 8: Get Your Act Together

Time to complete: 10 minutes to read, time to complete will vary
Activity: Complete Final Preparations Worksheet

You are in control of your mind and body; you are in charge of test anxiety, your preparation, and your test-taking strategies. Now it's time to take charge of external factors, like the testing site and the materials you need to take the exam.

Find Out Where the Test Is and Make a Trial Run

The USPS will tell you when and where your exam is being held. Do you know how to get to the testing site? Do you know how long it will take to get there? If not, make a trial run, preferably on the same day of the week at the same time of day. On the Final Preparations Worksheet, make note of the amount of time it will take you to get to the exam site. Plan on arriving 20–30 minutes early so you can get the lay of the land, use the bathroom, and calm down. Then, figure out how early you will have to get up that morning, and make sure you get up that early every day for a week before the exam.

Gather Your Materials

The night before the exam, lay out the clothes you will wear and the materials you have to bring with you to the exam. Plan on dressing in layers; you won't have any control over the temperature of the examination room. Have a sweater or jacket you can take off if it's warm. Use the checklist on the Final Preparations Worksheet to help you pull together what you will need.

Physical Preparation Checklist

For the week before the test, write down 1) what physical exercise you engaged in and for how long and 2) what you ate for each meal. Remember, you're trying for at least a half an hour of exercise every other day (preferably every day) and a balanced diet that's light on junk food.

Exam minus 7 days

Exercise: _____ for _____ minutes
Breakfast: _____
Lunch: _____
Dinner: _____
Snacks: _____

Exam minus 6 days

Exercise: _____ for _____ minutes
Breakfast: _____
Lunch: _____
Dinner: _____
Snacks: _____

Exam minus 5 days

Exercise: _____ for _____ minutes
Breakfast: _____
Lunch: _____
Dinner: _____
Snacks: _____

Exam minus 4 days

Exercise: _____ for _____ minutes
Breakfast: _____
Lunch: _____
Dinner: _____
Snacks: _____

Exam minus 3 days

Exercise: _____ for _____ minutes
Breakfast: _____
Lunch: _____
Dinner: _____
Snacks: _____

Exam minus 2 days

Exercise: _____ for _____ minutes
Breakfast: _____
Lunch: _____
Dinner: _____
Snacks: _____

Exam minus 1 day

Exercise: _____ for _____ minutes
Breakfast: _____
Lunch: _____
Dinner: _____
Snacks: _____

Eat Breakfast

Even if you don't usually eat breakfast, do so on exam morning. A cup of coffee doesn't count. Don't eat doughnuts or other sweet foods. A sugar high will leave you with a sugar low in the middle of the exam. A mix of protein and carbohydrates is best: Cereal with milk and just a little sugar or eggs with toast will do your body a world of good.

▶ Step 9: Do It!

**Time to complete: 10 minutes, plus test-taking time
Activity: Ace Test 473!**

Fast forward to exam day. You're ready. You made a study plan and followed through. You practiced your test-taking strategies while working through this book.

Final Preparations Worksheet

Getting to the Exam Site

Location of exam: _____

Date of exam: _____

Time of exam: _____

Do I know how to get to the exam site? Yes _____ No _____

If no, make a trial run.

Time it will take to get to exam site: _____

Things to Lay Out the Night before the Exam

Clothes I will wear   _____

Sweater/jacket   _____

Completed Sample Answer Sheet   _____

Admission card   _____

Photo ID   _____

Two No. 2 pencils   _____

_____   _____

_____   _____

You are in control of your physical, mental, and emotional state. You know when and where to show up and what to bring with you. In other words, you're better prepared than most of the other people taking the test with you. You are psyched.

Just one more thing. When you're done with Test 473, you will have earned a reward. Plan a celebration for exam night. Call up your friends and plan a party, have a nice dinner for two, or pick out a movie—whatever your heart desires. Give yourself something to look forward to.

And then do it. Complete Test 473, full of confidence, armed with test-taking strategies you've practiced until they're second nature. You're in control of yourself, your environment, and your performance on the exam. You're ready to succeed. So do it. Go in there and ace the exam. And look forward to your future career with the USPS!

▶ Practice Postal Worker Exam 1

CHAPTER SUMMARY

This is the first of the four practice exams based on Test 473 in this book, which the U.S. Postal Service uses to assess applicants for most entry-level jobs. Use this test to see how you would do if you had to take the exam today.

R emember that Test 473 has four parts (one part has two sections). Because Part D contains only questions that are based on your opinion and experience, it is not included in the practice tests in this book. To learn about these questions and to evaluate your responses, review Chapter 8.

Before you begin this test, find a quiet place to work and get your equipment together: some pencils for marking the answer grid and a stopwatch or alarm clock. Remember, each part of Test 473 is timed separately. Also make sure that you have enough time to complete the whole exam at one sitting—about an hour, including a few minutes' break between each part.

The answer sheet you should use for answering the questions is on pages 41–42. Then comes the exam itself, and after that is the answer key. The answer key is followed by a section on how to score your exam.

▶ Part A: Address Checking

1.	ⓐ	ⓑ	ⓒ	ⓓ
2.	ⓐ	ⓑ	ⓒ	ⓓ
3.	ⓐ	ⓑ	ⓒ	ⓓ
4.	ⓐ	ⓑ	ⓒ	ⓓ
5.	ⓐ	ⓑ	ⓒ	ⓓ
6.	ⓐ	ⓑ	ⓒ	ⓓ
7.	ⓐ	ⓑ	ⓒ	ⓓ
8.	ⓐ	ⓑ	ⓒ	ⓓ
9.	ⓐ	ⓑ	ⓒ	ⓓ
10.	ⓐ	ⓑ	ⓒ	ⓓ
11.	ⓐ	ⓑ	ⓒ	ⓓ
12.	ⓐ	ⓑ	ⓒ	ⓓ
13.	ⓐ	ⓑ	ⓒ	ⓓ
14.	ⓐ	ⓑ	ⓒ	ⓓ
15.	ⓐ	ⓑ	ⓒ	ⓓ
16.	ⓐ	ⓑ	ⓒ	ⓓ
17.	ⓐ	ⓑ	ⓒ	ⓓ
18.	ⓐ	ⓑ	ⓒ	ⓓ
19.	ⓐ	ⓑ	ⓒ	ⓓ
20.	ⓐ	ⓑ	ⓒ	ⓓ
21.	ⓐ	ⓑ	ⓒ	ⓓ
22.	ⓐ	ⓑ	ⓒ	ⓓ
23.	ⓐ	ⓑ	ⓒ	ⓓ
24.	ⓐ	ⓑ	ⓒ	ⓓ
25.	ⓐ	ⓑ	ⓒ	ⓓ
26.	ⓐ	ⓑ	ⓒ	ⓓ
27.	ⓐ	ⓑ	ⓒ	ⓓ
28.	ⓐ	ⓑ	ⓒ	ⓓ
29.	ⓐ	ⓑ	ⓒ	ⓓ
30.	ⓐ	ⓑ	ⓒ	ⓓ
31.	ⓐ	ⓑ	ⓒ	ⓓ
32.	ⓐ	ⓑ	ⓒ	ⓓ
33.	ⓐ	ⓑ	ⓒ	ⓓ
34.	ⓐ	ⓑ	ⓒ	ⓓ
35.	ⓐ	ⓑ	ⓒ	ⓓ
36.	ⓐ	ⓑ	ⓒ	ⓓ
37.	ⓐ	ⓑ	ⓒ	ⓓ
38.	ⓐ	ⓑ	ⓒ	ⓓ
39.	ⓐ	ⓑ	ⓒ	ⓓ
40.	ⓐ	ⓑ	ⓒ	ⓓ
41.	ⓐ	ⓑ	ⓒ	ⓓ
42.	ⓐ	ⓑ	ⓒ	ⓓ
43.	ⓐ	ⓑ	ⓒ	ⓓ
44.	ⓐ	ⓑ	ⓒ	ⓓ
45.	ⓐ	ⓑ	ⓒ	ⓓ
46.	ⓐ	ⓑ	ⓒ	ⓓ
47.	ⓐ	ⓑ	ⓒ	ⓓ
48.	ⓐ	ⓑ	ⓒ	ⓓ
49.	ⓐ	ⓑ	ⓒ	ⓓ
50.	ⓐ	ⓑ	ⓒ	ⓓ
51.	ⓐ	ⓑ	ⓒ	ⓓ
52.	ⓐ	ⓑ	ⓒ	ⓓ
53.	ⓐ	ⓑ	ⓒ	ⓓ
54.	ⓐ	ⓑ	ⓒ	ⓓ
55.	ⓐ	ⓑ	ⓒ	ⓓ
56.	ⓐ	ⓑ	ⓒ	ⓓ
57.	ⓐ	ⓑ	ⓒ	ⓓ
58.	ⓐ	ⓑ	ⓒ	ⓓ
59.	ⓐ	ⓑ	ⓒ	ⓓ
60.	ⓐ	ⓑ	ⓒ	ⓓ

▶ Part B: Forms Completion

1.	ⓐ	ⓑ	ⓒ	ⓓ
2.	ⓐ	ⓑ	ⓒ	ⓓ
3.	ⓐ	ⓑ	ⓒ	ⓓ
4.	ⓐ	ⓑ	ⓒ	ⓓ
5.	ⓐ	ⓑ	ⓒ	ⓓ
6.	ⓐ	ⓑ	ⓒ	ⓓ
7.	ⓐ	ⓑ	ⓒ	ⓓ
8.	ⓐ	ⓑ	ⓒ	ⓓ
9.	ⓐ	ⓑ	ⓒ	ⓓ
10.	ⓐ	ⓑ	ⓒ	ⓓ
11.	ⓐ	ⓑ	ⓒ	ⓓ
12.	ⓐ	ⓑ	ⓒ	ⓓ
13.	ⓐ	ⓑ	ⓒ	ⓓ
14.	ⓐ	ⓑ	ⓒ	ⓓ
15.	ⓐ	ⓑ	ⓒ	ⓓ
16.	ⓐ	ⓑ	ⓒ	ⓓ
17.	ⓐ	ⓑ	ⓒ	ⓓ
18.	ⓐ	ⓑ	ⓒ	ⓓ
19.	ⓐ	ⓑ	ⓒ	ⓓ
20.	ⓐ	ⓑ	ⓒ	ⓓ
21.	ⓐ	ⓑ	ⓒ	ⓓ
22.	ⓐ	ⓑ	ⓒ	ⓓ
23.	ⓐ	ⓑ	ⓒ	ⓓ
24.	ⓐ	ⓑ	ⓒ	ⓓ
25.	ⓐ	ⓑ	ⓒ	ⓓ
26.	ⓐ	ⓑ	ⓒ	ⓓ
27.	ⓐ	ⓑ	ⓒ	ⓓ
28.	ⓐ	ⓑ	ⓒ	ⓓ
29.	ⓐ	ⓑ	ⓒ	ⓓ
30.	ⓐ	ⓑ	ⓒ	ⓓ

▶ Part C: Section 1—Coding

1.	ⓐ	ⓑ	ⓒ	ⓓ	13.	ⓐ	ⓑ	ⓒ	ⓓ	25.	ⓐ	ⓑ	ⓒ	ⓓ
2.	ⓐ	ⓑ	ⓒ	ⓓ	14.	ⓐ	ⓑ	ⓒ	ⓓ	26.	ⓐ	ⓑ	ⓒ	ⓓ
3.	ⓐ	ⓑ	ⓒ	ⓓ	15.	ⓐ	ⓑ	ⓒ	ⓓ	27.	ⓐ	ⓑ	ⓒ	ⓓ
4.	ⓐ	ⓑ	ⓒ	ⓓ	16.	ⓐ	ⓑ	ⓒ	ⓓ	28.	ⓐ	ⓑ	ⓒ	ⓓ
5.	ⓐ	ⓑ	ⓒ	ⓓ	17.	ⓐ	ⓑ	ⓒ	ⓓ	29.	ⓐ	ⓑ	ⓒ	ⓓ
6.	ⓐ	ⓑ	ⓒ	ⓓ	18.	ⓐ	ⓑ	ⓒ	ⓓ	30.	ⓐ	ⓑ	ⓒ	ⓓ
7.	ⓐ	ⓑ	ⓒ	ⓓ	19.	ⓐ	ⓑ	ⓒ	ⓓ	31.	ⓐ	ⓑ	ⓒ	ⓓ
8.	ⓐ	ⓑ	ⓒ	ⓓ	20.	ⓐ	ⓑ	ⓒ	ⓓ	32.	ⓐ	ⓑ	ⓒ	ⓓ
9.	ⓐ	ⓑ	ⓒ	ⓓ	21.	ⓐ	ⓑ	ⓒ	ⓓ	33.	ⓐ	ⓑ	ⓒ	ⓓ
10.	ⓐ	ⓑ	ⓒ	ⓓ	22.	ⓐ	ⓑ	ⓒ	ⓓ	34.	ⓐ	ⓑ	ⓒ	ⓓ
11.	ⓐ	ⓑ	ⓒ	ⓓ	23.	ⓐ	ⓑ	ⓒ	ⓓ	35.	ⓐ	ⓑ	ⓒ	ⓓ
12.	ⓐ	ⓑ	ⓒ	ⓓ	24.	ⓐ	ⓑ	ⓒ	ⓓ	36.	ⓐ	ⓑ	ⓒ	ⓓ

▶ Part C: Section 2—Memory

37.	ⓐ	ⓑ	ⓒ	ⓓ	49.	ⓐ	ⓑ	ⓒ	ⓓ	61.	ⓐ	ⓑ	ⓒ	ⓓ
38.	ⓐ	ⓑ	ⓒ	ⓓ	50.	ⓐ	ⓑ	ⓒ	ⓓ	62.	ⓐ	ⓑ	ⓒ	ⓓ
39.	ⓐ	ⓑ	ⓒ	ⓓ	51.	ⓐ	ⓑ	ⓒ	ⓓ	63.	ⓐ	ⓑ	ⓒ	ⓓ
40.	ⓐ	ⓑ	ⓒ	ⓓ	52.	ⓐ	ⓑ	ⓒ	ⓓ	64.	ⓐ	ⓑ	ⓒ	ⓓ
41.	ⓐ	ⓑ	ⓒ	ⓓ	53.	ⓐ	ⓑ	ⓒ	ⓓ	65.	ⓐ	ⓑ	ⓒ	ⓓ
42.	ⓐ	ⓑ	ⓒ	ⓓ	54.	ⓐ	ⓑ	ⓒ	ⓓ	66.	ⓐ	ⓑ	ⓒ	ⓓ
43.	ⓐ	ⓑ	ⓒ	ⓓ	55.	ⓐ	ⓑ	ⓒ	ⓓ	67.	ⓐ	ⓑ	ⓒ	ⓓ
44.	ⓐ	ⓑ	ⓒ	ⓓ	56.	ⓐ	ⓑ	ⓒ	ⓓ	68.	ⓐ	ⓑ	ⓒ	ⓓ
45.	ⓐ	ⓑ	ⓒ	ⓓ	57.	ⓐ	ⓑ	ⓒ	ⓓ	69.	ⓐ	ⓑ	ⓒ	ⓓ
46.	ⓐ	ⓑ	ⓒ	ⓓ	58.	ⓐ	ⓑ	ⓒ	ⓓ	70.	ⓐ	ⓑ	ⓒ	ⓓ
47.	ⓐ	ⓑ	ⓒ	ⓓ	59.	ⓐ	ⓑ	ⓒ	ⓓ	71.	ⓐ	ⓑ	ⓒ	ⓓ
48.	ⓐ	ⓑ	ⓒ	ⓓ	60.	ⓐ	ⓑ	ⓒ	ⓓ	72.	ⓐ	ⓑ	ⓒ	ⓓ

▶ Practice Postal Worker Exam 1

Part A—Address Checking

Directions: Review and compare the information in the **List to Be Checked** with the information in the **Correct List**. To answer each question, you must decide if there are **No errors (a)**, an error in the **Address only (b)**, an error in the **ZIP code only (c)**, or an error in **Both (d)** the address and the ZIP code. This part has 60 questions.

Time: 11 minutes

	CORRECT LIST		LIST TO BE CHECKED	
QUESTION	**ADDRESS**	**ZIP CODE**	**ADDRESS**	**ZIP CODE**
1.	1617 Ellis Dr Jonesville, LA	71343-9643	1617 Ellis Dr Jonesville, LA	71343-9643
2.	2517 Holiday Rd Kaiser, MO	65047	2617 Holiday Rd Kaiser, MO	65047
3.	1153 Grand Road Jenner, CA	95450	1153 Grant Road Jenner, CA	95440
4.	2821 Wesleyan Ln. Highland, NY	12528-7483	2821 Wellesley Ln. Highland, NY	12528-7483
5.	4745 Schooner Boulevard Jacob, FL	32431-2653	4745 Schooner Boulevard Jacob, FL	32431-2653
6.	1906 Rochester Ct Island Falls, ME	04747	1906 Rochester Ct Island Falls, MN	04747
7.	2228 Richards Dr Leeper, PA	16233	2228 Richards Dr Leeper, PA	16223
8.	608 South 5th St Lyme, CT	06371-2674	608 South 6th St Lyme, CT	06371-2674
9.	1339 Teeters Court Means, KY	40346	1339 Teeters Court Means, KS	40336
10.	2519 Aster Av Mount Wolf, PA	17347	2519 Aster Av Wolf Mountain, PA	17374
11.	2334 Canal Road New River, VA	24129	2334 Canal Road New River, VA	24129

a. No errors
b. Address only
c. ZIP code only
d. Both

	CORRECT LIST		LIST TO BE CHECKED	
QUESTION	**ADDRESS**	**ZIP CODE**	**ADDRESS**	**ZIP CODE**
12.	87 East 23rd Street Novelty, MO	63460-0098	87 East 23rd Street Novelty, MO	63460-0998
13.	2318 Ridgeland Hwy Nye, MT	59061	2318 Ridgeland Hwy Rye, MN	59061
14.	8856 Kennedy Pk Raymond, KS	67573-6836	8556 Kennedy Pk Raymond, KS	67573-6836
15.	732 Moorefield Street Quincy, MI	49802	732 Moorefield Street Quincy, MI	49802
16.	1728 Gleason Av Putnam, TX	76469	1728 Gleason Av Putnam, TX	76469
17.	3546 Bedell St Ranier, MN	56668-5342	3456 Bedell St Ranier, MN	56688-5342
18.	3434 Greenleaf Street Smyrna, DE	19977	3434 Greenleaf Street Smyrna, DE	19777
19.	7471 Pine Island Road Moorhead, IA	51558	7471 Pine Island Road Moorhead, IL	51588
20.	1111 More Road Hedgesville, WV	25427-8724	1111 Moore Road Hedgesville, WV	25427-8724
21.	4858 Cumberland Boulevard Herald, CA	95638	4888 Cumberland Boulevard Herald, CA	95630
22.	21 Westview Dr Leal, ND	58479	211 Westview Dr Leal, ND	54879
23.	5042 Colfax Ave N Mecca, IN	47860	5042 Colfax Lane N Mecca, IN	47860
24.	1492 Bridgeton Road Randle, WA	98377	1492 Bridgeton Road Randle, WA	98337
25.	1807 S Gilbert Dr Slinger, WI	53086	1807 S Gilbert Dr Singer, WI	53068

a. No errors
b. Address only
c. ZIP code only
d. Both

QUESTION	CORRECT LIST ADDRESS	ZIP CODE	LIST TO BE CHECKED ADDRESS	ZIP CODE
26.	801 Yale Avenue Venus, FL	33960	801 Yale Avenue Venus, FL	33960
27.	6619 10th Street Upsala, MN	56384-0019	6619 10th Street Upsala, MS	56384-0009
28.	515 Summit Avenue NW Vandalia, IL	62471	515 Summit Avenue SW Vandalia, IL	62471
29.	1133 Apple Way Whatley, AL	36482	1133 Apple Way Whatley, AL	63482
30.	21 Old Pelham Rd W Yatahey, NM	87375	21 Old Pelling Rd W Yatahey, NM	87575
31.	2450 Bittersweet Ct Zwolle, LA	71486	2460 Bittersweet Ct Zwolle, LA	71486
32.	8014 Bobcat Cir Rogers, AR	72756-6873	8014 Bobcat Cir Rogers, AR	72756-6873
33.	3756 Sessions Drive Petersham, MA	01366	3756 Seasons Drive Peterson, MA	03166
34.	2630 Thrush Pl Mozier, IL	62070	2600 Thrush Pl Mozier, IL	62007
35.	5002 Clonmel Road Lanexa, VA	23089	5002 Clonmel Road Lanexa, MA	23089
36.	4018 Quentin Road Jay, OK	74346-2534	4018 Quincy Road Jay, OK	74346-2544
37.	432 N Southfields Ave Kalskag, AK	99607	432 N Southfields Ave Kalskag, AK	99007
38.	4365 Country Lane Foxholm, ND	58718	4365 County Lane Foxholm, ND	58719
39.	86 Toms River Rd Capitola, CA	95010	86 Toms River Rd Capitola, CA	95110

a. No errors
b. Address only
c. ZIP code only
d. Both

QUESTION	CORRECT LIST		LIST TO BE CHECKED	
	ADDRESS	ZIP CODE	ADDRESS	ZIP CODE
40.	4241 Applegate St Arvada, WY	82831-7667	4241 Applegate St Arvada, WY	82831-7667
41.	7801 Foxcove Ct Berkey, OH	43504	7801 Foxcove Ct Berkeley, OH	34504
42.	1211 Bella Vista Place Chaska, MN	55318	1211 Bella Vista Place Chaska, MN	53318
43.	3319 Middle Rd Milan, NH	03588	3319 Middle Dr Milan, NH	03588
44.	3926 Nolensville Road New Point, IN	47263-9524	3926 Nolensville Road New Point, IN	47263-9524
45.	7846 Birchwood Pl Perry, UT	84302	7846 Birchwood Ln Perry, UT	84302
46.	2514 Flint St Fleet, VA	23511	2514 Flint St Flint, VA	23511
47.	3314 Riverside Rd SE Hill, NH	03243	3314 Riverside Dr SE Hill, ND	03343
48.	3817 Litchfield Rd Pueblo, CO	81001	3817 Litchfield Rd Pueblo, CO	81001
49.	1292 Hastings Ln Rush, KY	41168-5284	1292 Hastings Ln Rush, KY	41168-5248
50.	7117 Whitney Av Magnetic Springs, OH	43036	7117 Whitney Av Majestic Springs, OH	43036
51.	2514 Crystal Terrace Jenkins, MO	65605	2514 Crystal Terrace Jenkins, MO	65506
52.	4950 Hunts Hill Road Flomot, TX	79234	4950 Hunts Hill Road Flomot, TX	79234
53.	1418 Sugar Creek Circle Elk Horn, ID	83354	1418 Sugar Creek Court Elk Horn, ID	83354

a. No errors
b. Address only
c. ZIP code only
d. Both

	CORRECT LIST		LIST TO BE CHECKED	
QUESTION	ADDRESS	ZIP CODE	ADDRESS	ZIP CODE
54.	6872 S Summit Street Capels, WV	24820-5533	6872 S Summit Street Capels, WA	24820-5533
55.	4774 Roosevelt Terrace Ash Flat, AR	72513	4774 Roosevelt Terrace Ash Flat, AR	72513
56.	1909 Seashore Ave Curwensville, PA	16833	1900 Seashore Ave Curwensville, PA	16383
57.	9813 Heather Pl Igo, CA	96047	9813 Heather Ln Igo, CA	90047
58.	2020 Brackett Place Huntland, TN	37345	2020 Brackett Place Huntland, TN	37355
59.	2756 Rosemont Boulevard Mead, CO	80542-6278	2756 Rosevelt Boulevard Mead, CO	80542-6278
60.	9818 Spring Dr Penokee, KS	67659	9818 Spring Dr Penokee, KS	67659

a. No errors
b. Address only
c. ZIP code only
d. Both

Part B—Forms Completion

Directions: Review each form and answer the 30 questions that follow.

Time: 15 minutes

Return Receipt

Completed by Sender		Completed by Recipient
1a. Sender's Name		A. Last Name
1b. Recipient's Name		B. First Name
		C. Signature
2a. Address		D. Date received
2b. City		E. Number of items received
2c. State		[ ] 1 [ ] 6
2d. ZIP Code		[ ] 2 [ ] 7
		[ ] 3 [ ] 8
3a. Signature of Sender	3b. Date	[ ] 4 [ ] 9
		[ ] 5 [ ] 10
		[ ] 11 or more

1. Which is completed by the sender?
   a. boxes 1 and 2 only
   b. all numbered boxes
   c. all lettered boxes
   d. boxes A, B, and C only

2. A recipient's name belongs in which of the following boxes?
   a. A
   b. 2
   c. 2a
   d. 1b

3. You could expect to find "11/15/09" in which of the following boxes?
   a. 3b only
   b. D only
   c. E
   d. 3b and D

4. Which would be a correct entry for box 2d?
   a. 91941
   b. 9/8/09
   c. Arizona
   d. Jori Sinclair

5. How many check marks should there be on this receipt?
a. 1
b. 2
c. 3
d. 4

6. If the recipient receives 12 packages, which box would contain a check mark?
a. A
b. 3a
c. E
d. D

7. Which box indicates the destination city of the package?
a. 2a
b. 2b
c. 2c
d. 3a

8. How many boxes must the recipient complete?
a. 4
b. 5
c. 6
d. 7

9. You could expect to see "3567 Northern Road" in which box?
a. 1a
b. 2a
c. 2b
d. 2c

10. How many signatures are required to complete this form?
a. 0
b. 1
c. 2
d. 4

Origination Form

1. ZIP Code	5. Scheduled Time of Delivery	6. Postage $
	(a) Noon	7. COD Fee $
2. Date Accepted (a) Mo. _____ (b) Day _____ (c) Year _____	(b) 3 PM	8. Insurance Fee $
	(c) Other	9. Return Receipt Fee $
3. Time Accepted (a) _____ AM (b) _____ PM		10. Total Postage and Fees $
4. Postage Rate (a) Flat Rate [ ] (b) Weight [ ] (i) _____ lbs (ii) _____ ozs		11. Signature
		12. Date

11. The name "Melinda Soo" could be found in which of the following boxes?
   a. 4
   b. 8
   c. 10
   d. 11

12. If a package is not weighed to rate postage, which box is checked?
   a. 3a
   b. 3b
   c. 4a
   d. 4b

13. Which boxes indicate dates?
   a. 2 only
   b. 3 only
   c. 2 and 3
   d. 2 and 12

14. Which box would contain "85713"?
   a. 1
   b. 2
   c. 3
   d. 4

15. What is the total number of specified fees indicated on this form?
   a. 1
   b. 2
   c. 3
   d. 4

16. The year a package is accepted should be written in which line?
   a. 2c
   b. 3a
   c. 4b
   d. 11

17. Which line would indicate a 10-pound package?

   a. 3a

   b. 4a

   c. 4bi

   d. 4bii

18. After adding the postage and fees, where would you write the total?

   a. box 6

   b. box 7

   c. box 10

   d. box 12

19. Which box indicates how the postage rate is calculated?

   a. 1

   b. 4

   c. 6

   d. 10

20. Which of the following would be selected if a 11 A.M. delivery is scheduled?

   a. 5

   b. 5a

   c. 5b

   d. 5c

Merchandise Return Receipt

1. Description of Merchandise	4. Last Name
1A. Number of Items	5. First Name
2. Weight A. lbs B. ozs	6. Postage
	7. Handling Fees
3. Postmark	8. Total Postage and Fees
	9. Date of Receipt A. Day B. Mo. C. Year
	10. Signature Waiver [ ] Yes [ ] No
	11. Signature 12. Date

21. Which box contains the postmark?
   a. 3
   b. 6
   c. 8
   d. 9

22. Besides postage, what other fees are included on the receipt?
   a. COD fees
   b. handling fees
   c. insurance fees
   d. tax

23. To show a package is more than four pounds, which line should be filled in?
   a. 1A
   b. 2A
   c. 2B
   d. 9A

24. If postage is $2 and handling is $2, in which box would you enter $4?
   a. 2
   b. 6
   c. 7
   d. 8

25. If the package is received on January 7, 2009, what number belongs in line 9B?
   a. 1
   b. 7
   c. 07
   d. 2009

26. To indicate a waived signature, which box must be completed?
   a. 8
   b. 9
   c. 10
   d. 11

27. Which boxes tell the dates a package was received?
- **a.** 2, 10
- **b.** 9, 10
- **c.** 10, 11
- **d.** 9, 12

28. In which box would you likely find the words "promotional T-shirts"?
- **a.** 1
- **b.** 1a
- **c.** 2
- **d.** 3

29. If there are no handling fees, box 8 is the same as which box?
- **a.** 6
- **b.** 7
- **c.** 8
- **d.** 9

30. Box 1A contains which of the following?
- **a.** description of merchandise
- **b.** last name
- **c.** number of items
- **d.** weight

Part C, Section 1—Coding

Directions: Read and review the Coding Guide. Each of the 36 questions offers an **Address**. Choose which **Delivery Route** each address belongs in according to the Coding Guide.

Time: 6 minutes

CODING GUIDE	
ADDRESS RANGE	**DELIVERY ROUTE**
101–200 Biltmore Lane 50–300 Foothill Ave 1–19 W 54th Street	A
201–300 Biltmore Lane 20–29 W 54th Street	B
9500–10500 Oliver Ave 1–15 Highway Route 7 301–3400 Foothill Ave	C
All mail that doesn't belong in one of the address ranges listed here.	D

1. 110 Billmore Lane
  a. Delivery Route A
  b. Delivery Route B
  c. Delivery Route C
  d. Delivery Route D

2. 9555 Oliver Ave
  a. Delivery Route A
  b. Delivery Route B
  c. Delivery Route C
  d. Delivery Route D

3. 17 W 54th Street
  a. Delivery Route A
  b. Delivery Route B
  c. Delivery Route C
  d. Delivery Route D

4. 230 Biltmore Lane
  a. Delivery Route A
  b. Delivery Route B
  c. Delivery Route C
  d. Delivery Route D

5. 7 Highway Route 7
  a. Delivery Route A
  b. Delivery Route B
  c. Delivery Route C
  d. Delivery Route D

6. 100 Biltmore Lane
  a. Delivery Route A
  b. Delivery Route B
  c. Delivery Route C
  d. Delivery Route D

7. 75 Foothill Ave
   a. Delivery Route A
   b. Delivery Route B
   c. Delivery Route C
   d. Delivery Route D

8. 299 Biltmore Drive
   a. Delivery Route A
   b. Delivery Route B
   c. Delivery Route C
   d. Delivery Route D

9. 30 W 54th Street
   a. Delivery Route A
   b. Delivery Route B
   c. Delivery Route C
   d. Delivery Route D

10. 204 Biltmore Lane
   a. Delivery Route A
   b. Delivery Route B
   c. Delivery Route C
   d. Delivery Route D

11. 89 Foothill Ave
   a. Delivery Route A
   b. Delivery Route B
   c. Delivery Route C
   d. Delivery Route D

12. 14 Highway Route 9
   a. Delivery Route A
   b. Delivery Route B
   c. Delivery Route C
   d. Delivery Route D

13. 3230 Foothill Dr
   a. Delivery Route A
   b. Delivery Route B
   c. Delivery Route C
   d. Delivery Route D

14. 23 W 54th Street
   a. Delivery Route A
   b. Delivery Route B
   c. Delivery Route C
   d. Delivery Route D

15. 49 Foothill Ave
   a. Delivery Route A
   b. Delivery Route B
   c. Delivery Route C
   d. Delivery Route D

16. 10001 Olive Ave
   a. Delivery Route A
   b. Delivery Route B
   c. Delivery Route C
   d. Delivery Route D

17. 340 Foothill Ave
   a. Delivery Route A
   b. Delivery Route B
   c. Delivery Route C
   d. Delivery Route D

18. 12 W 54th Street
   a. Delivery Route A
   b. Delivery Route B
   c. Delivery Route C
   d. Delivery Route D

19. 2 Highway Route 7
   a. Delivery Route A
   b. Delivery Route B
   c. Delivery Route C
   d. Delivery Route D

20. 287 Biltmore Way
   a. Delivery Route A
   b. Delivery Route B
   c. Delivery Route C
   d. Delivery Route D

21. 19 W 54th Street
   a. Delivery Route A
   b. Delivery Route B
   c. Delivery Route C
   d. Delivery Route D

22. 3333 Foothill Ave
   a. Delivery Route A
   b. Delivery Route B
   c. Delivery Route C
   d. Delivery Route D

23. 13 W 54th Street
   a. Delivery Route A
   b. Delivery Route B
   c. Delivery Route C
   d. Delivery Route D

24. 221 Biltmore Lane
   a. Delivery Route A
   b. Delivery Route B
   c. Delivery Route C
   d. Delivery Route D

25. 9633 Oliver Blvd
   a. Delivery Route A
   b. Delivery Route B
   c. Delivery Route C
   d. Delivery Route D

26. 18 Highway Route 7
   a. Delivery Route A
   b. Delivery Route B
   c. Delivery Route C
   d. Delivery Route D

27. 200 Biltmore Lane
   a. Delivery Route A
   b. Delivery Route B
   c. Delivery Route C
   d. Delivery Route D

28. 22 W 54th Street
   a. Delivery Route A
   b. Delivery Route B
   c. Delivery Route C
   d. Delivery Route D

29. 256 Biltmore Lane
   a. Delivery Route A
   b. Delivery Route B
   c. Delivery Route C
   d. Delivery Route D

30. 9550 Oliver Ave
   a. Delivery Route A
   b. Delivery Route B
   c. Delivery Route C
   d. Delivery Route D

31. 3399 Foothill Ave
   a. Delivery Route A
   b. Delivery Route B
   c. Delivery Route C
   d. Delivery Route D

32. 202 Biltmore Lane
   a. Delivery Route A
   b. Delivery Route B
   c. Delivery Route C
   d. Delivery Route D

33. 18 W 54th Street
   a. Delivery Route A
   b. Delivery Route B
   c. Delivery Route C
   d. Delivery Route D

34. 270 Foothill Ave
   a. Delivery Route A
   b. Delivery Route B
   c. Delivery Route C
   d. Delivery Route D

35. 8 Highway Route 7
   a. Delivery Route A
   b. Delivery Route B
   c. Delivery Route C
   d. Delivery Route D

36. 21 W 54th Street
   a. Delivery Route A
   b. Delivery Route B
   c. Delivery Route C
   d. Delivery Route D

Part C, Section 2—Memory

Directions: Spend three minutes memorizing the information found in the **Coding Guide**. You may NOT take any notes during this time. Next, you will answer the 72 questions. Each question offers an **Address**. Choose which **Delivery Route** each address belongs in according to your memory of the Coding Guide. **Note: You may NOT turn back to the page displaying the Coding Guide once the Memory section has begun.**

Time: 3 minutes for memorization, 7 minutes to answer questions

CODING GUIDE	
ADDRESS RANGE	**DELIVERY ROUTE**
101–200 Biltmore Lane 50–300 Foothill Ave 1–19 W 54th Street	A
201–300 Biltmore Lane 20–29 W 54th Street	B
9500–10500 Oliver Ave 1–15 Highway Route 7 301–3400 Foothill Ave	C
All mail that doesn't belong in one of the address ranges listed here.	D

37. 3330 Fonthill Ave
   a. Delivery Route A
   b. Delivery Route B
   c. Delivery Route C
   d. Delivery Route D

38. 9600 Oliver Ave
   a. Delivery Route A
   b. Delivery Route B
   c. Delivery Route C
   d. Delivery Route D

39. 15 W 54th Street
   a. Delivery Route A
   b. Delivery Route B
   c. Delivery Route C
   d. Delivery Route D

40. 11 Highway Route 17
   a. Delivery Route A
   b. Delivery Route B
   c. Delivery Route C
   d. Delivery Route D

41. 340 Foothill Ave
   a. Delivery Route A
   b. Delivery Route B
   c. Delivery Route C
   d. Delivery Route D

42. 26 W 54th Street
   a. Delivery Route A
   b. Delivery Route B
   c. Delivery Route C
   d. Delivery Route D

43. 80 Foothill Ave
   a. Delivery Route A
   b. Delivery Route B
   c. Delivery Route C
   d. Delivery Route D

44. 9800 Oliver Ave
   a. Delivery Route A
   b. Delivery Route B
   c. Delivery Route C
   d. Delivery Route D

45. 27 Highway Route 7
   a. Delivery Route A
   b. Delivery Route B
   c. Delivery Route C
   d. Delivery Route D

46. 370 Biltmore Lane
   a. Delivery Route A
   b. Delivery Route B
   c. Delivery Route C
   d. Delivery Route D

47. 3 W 54th Street
   a. Delivery Route A
   b. Delivery Route B
   c. Delivery Route C
   d. Delivery Route D

48. 19 E 54th Street
   a. Delivery Route A
   b. Delivery Route B
   c. Delivery Route C
   d. Delivery Route D

49. 150 Foothill Ave
   a. Delivery Route A
   b. Delivery Route B
   c. Delivery Route C
   d. Delivery Route D

50. 10000 Oliver Ave
   a. Delivery Route A
   b. Delivery Route B
   c. Delivery Route C
   d. Delivery Route D

51. 24 W 54th Street
   a. Delivery Route A
   b. Delivery Route B
   c. Delivery Route C
   d. Delivery Route D

52. 3550 Foothill Ave
   a. Delivery Route A
   b. Delivery Route B
   c. Delivery Route C
   d. Delivery Route D

53. 166 Biltmore Lane
   a. Delivery Route A
   b. Delivery Route B
   c. Delivery Route C
   d. Delivery Route D

54. 280 Biltmore Lane
   a. Delivery Route A
   b. Delivery Route B
   c. Delivery Route C
   d. Delivery Route D

55. 4 W 54th Street
   a. Delivery Route A
   b. Delivery Route B
   c. Delivery Route C
   d. Delivery Route D

56. 29 Highway Route 7
   a. Delivery Route A
   b. Delivery Route B
   c. Delivery Route C
   d. Delivery Route D

57. 290 Biltmore Lane
   a. Delivery Route A
   b. Delivery Route B
   c. Delivery Route C
   d. Delivery Route D

58. 480 Fontville Ave
   a. Delivery Route A
   b. Delivery Route B
   c. Delivery Route C
   d. Delivery Route D

59. 11 Highway Route 7
   a. Delivery Route A
   b. Delivery Route B
   c. Delivery Route C
   d. Delivery Route D

60. 10 Biltmore Lane
   a. Delivery Route A
   b. Delivery Route B
   c. Delivery Route C
   d. Delivery Route D

61. 230 Foothill Ave
   a. Delivery Route A
   b. Delivery Route B
   c. Delivery Route C
   d. Delivery Route D

62. 9650 Oliver Ave
   a. Delivery Route A
   b. Delivery Route B
   c. Delivery Route C
   d. Delivery Route D

63. 21 W 54th Street
   a. Delivery Route A
   b. Delivery Route B
   c. Delivery Route C
   d. Delivery Route D

64. 158 Foothill Ave
   a. Delivery Route A
   b. Delivery Route B
   c. Delivery Route C
   d. Delivery Route D

65. 10100 Oliver Ave
   a. Delivery Route A
   b. Delivery Route B
   c. Delivery Route C
   d. Delivery Route D

66. 296 Biltmore Lane
   a. Delivery Route A
   b. Delivery Route B
   c. Delivery Route C
   d. Delivery Route D

67. 14 Biltmore Lane
   a. Delivery Route A
   b. Delivery Route B
   c. Delivery Route C
   d. Delivery Route D

68. 4 Highway Route 7
   a. Delivery Route A
   b. Delivery Route B
   c. Delivery Route C
   d. Delivery Route D

69. 81 Foothill Ave
   a. Delivery Route A
   b. Delivery Route B
   c. Delivery Route C
   d. Delivery Route D

70. 20 W 54th Street
   a. Delivery Route A
   b. Delivery Route B
   c. Delivery Route C
   d. Delivery Route D

71. 11 Highway Road 7
   a. Delivery Route A
   b. Delivery Route B
   c. Delivery Route C
   d. Delivery Route D

72. 800 Foothill Ave
   a. Delivery Route A
   b. Delivery Route B
   c. Delivery Route C
   d. Delivery Route D

▶ Answers

Part A—Address Checking

1. a.	**16.** a.	**31.** b.	**46.** b.
2. b.	**17.** d.	**32.** a.	**47.** d.
3. d.	**18.** c.	**33.** d.	**48.** a.
4. b.	**19.** d.	**34.** d.	**49.** c.
5. a.	**20.** b.	**35.** b.	**50.** b.
6. b.	**21.** d.	**36.** d.	**51.** c.
7. c.	**22.** d.	**37.** c.	**52.** a.
8. b.	**23.** b.	**38.** d.	**53.** b.
9. d.	**24.** c.	**39.** c.	**54.** b.
10. d.	**25.** d.	**40.** a.	**55.** a.
11. a.	**26.** a.	**41.** d.	**56.** d.
12. c.	**27.** d.	**42.** c.	**57.** d.
13. b.	**28.** b.	**43.** b.	**58.** c.
14. b.	**29.** c.	**44.** a.	**59.** b.
15. a.	**30.** d.	**45.** b.	**60.** a.

Part B—Forms Completion

1. b. The left side of the form, all numbered boxes, is labeled "Completed by Sender."

2. d. Box 1b is for the recipient's name.

3. d. "11/15/09" is a date, so it belongs in any box labeled for a date; in this case, boxes 3b and D require dates.

4. a. Box 2d is labeled "ZIP code." Therefore, 91941 is correct.

5. a. There can be only one number of items received; therefore, there should be only one check mark in box E.

6. c. Box E shows the number of items received, so it would contain a check mark.

7. b. Only box 2b on this form requires a city's name.

8. b. The recipient must fill out all the lettered boxes on the right hand side of the form. There are five lettered boxes.

9. b. The address belongs in box 2a; therefore, **b** is the correct answer.

10. c. This form requires the sender's signature and the recipient's signature; therefore, the answer is 2.

11. d. Only box 11 requires a signature, which would include a name.

12. c. The key word here is *rate*. Box 4 shows the rate. If a weight is not included, then the package must be sent at a flat rate, choice **c**.

13. d. On this form, two dates are indicated: one when the package is accepted and the other when the form is signed.

14. a. This number is a standard ZIP code and belongs in box 1.

15. c. There are three fees specified: COD fee, insurance fee, and return receipt fee.

16. a. Look at box 2. The year a package is accepted is listed in line 2c.

17. c. Weight is listed in box 4 only. Pounds are found on line 4bi.

18. c. The total postage and fees should be listed in box 10.

19. b. Box 4 indicates the rate, so **b** is the correct answer.

20. d. Box 5 indicates the scheduled time of delivery. Since "11 A.M." is not one of the choices, "other" (5c) must be selected.

21. a. The postmark belongs in box 3.

22. b. The only box to indicate fees is box 7, handling fees.

23. b. Box 2A shows weight in pounds.

24. d. Box 8 shows the total postage and fees.

25. a. Line 9B indicates the month. January is the first month, so that line should include a 1.

26. c. The signature waiver appears in box 10.

27. d. The date of receipt and the date of signature are both required to complete this form.

28. a. Box 1 requires a description of the merchandise being returned. It is likely that this is the description of the items and, therefore, belongs in box 1.

29. a. Box 8 shows the total postage and handling fees. If there are no handling fees, then the total postage and fees (box 8) is the same as the postage (box 6).

30. c. Box 1A contains the number of items being returned.

Part C, Section 1—Coding

1. d.	**10.** b.	**19.** c.	**28.** b.
2. c.	**11.** a.	**20.** d.	**29.** b.
3. a.	**12.** d.	**21.** a.	**30.** c.
4. b.	**13.** d.	**22.** c.	**31.** c.
5. c.	**14.** b.	**23.** a.	**32.** b.
6. d.	**15.** d.	**24.** b.	**33.** a.
7. a.	**16.** d.	**25.** d.	**34.** a.
8. d.	**17.** c.	**26.** d.	**35.** c.
9. d.	**18.** a.	**27.** a.	**36.** b.

Part C, Section 2—Memory

37. d.	**46.** d.	**55.** a.	**64.** a.
38. c.	**47.** a.	**56.** d.	**65.** c.
39. a.	**48.** d.	**57.** b.	**66.** b.
40. d.	**49.** a.	**58.** d.	**67.** d.
41. c.	**50.** c.	**59.** c.	**68.** c.
42. b.	**51.** b.	**60.** d.	**69.** a.
43. a.	**52.** d.	**61.** a.	**70.** b.
44. c.	**53.** a.	**62.** c.	**71.** d.
45. d.	**54.** b.	**63.** b.	**72.** c.

▶ Scoring

The USPS uses a complicated formula to convert your raw score—the number of questions you got right, minus a fraction of the number you got wrong for some parts of the exam—to your basic rating. The basic rating is on a scale of 1 to 100, and that's the score the USPS will use to rank you against other applicants. To help gauge your success on this practice exam, start by calculating your raw score.

Your Raw Score

Here's how to determine your raw score for each part.

Part A—Address Checking

First, count the questions you got right. Then, count the number of questions you got wrong. Questions you didn't answer don't count either way. Don't forget to multiply the questions you got wrong by $\frac{1}{3}$.

1. Number of questions right: _____
2. Number of questions wrong: _____
3. Number of questions wrong
   multiplied by $\frac{1}{3}$: _____
4. Subtract number 3 from number 1: _____

The result in line 4 is your raw score on Part A.

Part B—Forms Completion

Count the questions you got right. Questions you got wrong or didn't answer don't count either way.

Number of questions right: _____

The result is your raw score on Part B.

Part C, Section 1—Coding

First, count the questions you got right. Then, count the number of questions you got wrong. Questions you didn't answer don't count either way. Don't forget to multiply the questions you got wrong by $\frac{1}{3}$.

1. Number of questions right: _____
2. Number of questions wrong: _____
3. Number of questions wrong
   multiplied by $\frac{1}{3}$: _____
4. Subtract number 3 from number 1: _____

The result in line 4 is your raw score on this section of Part C.

Part C, Section 2—Memory

First, count the questions you got right. Then, count the number of questions you got wrong. Questions you didn't answer don't count either way. Don't forget to multiply the questions you got wrong by $\frac{1}{3}$.

1. Number of questions right: _____
2. Number of questions wrong: _____
3. Number of questions wrong
   multiplied by $\frac{1}{3}$: _____
4. Subtract number 3 from number 1: _____

The result in line 4 is your raw score on this section of Part C.

Part D—Personal Characteristics and Experience Inventory

Remember, there are no right or wrong answers on this section of Test 473 and these questions appear only once in Chapter 8. In addition, the USPS has not released information on how your responses to the questions are "scored." For these reasons, Part D is not used to calculate your raw score on this practice exam.

Total Raw Score

For your total raw score, add together the four raw scores you just calculated.

Total raw score: _____

Basic Rating

To calculate your basic rating, the USPS converts your raw scores on Parts A, B, and C and factors in the results of Part D. As aforementioned, the basic rating is based on a scale of 1 to 100 with 70 being the required passing score to be eligible for a job with the USPS. It is very difficult to give you an accurate basic rating based on this practice exam; however, if your raw score on this practice test is above 100, you are on your way to passing the official exam.

▶ The Next Step

If your score isn't where you want it to be, do not give up. Test 473 is a tough exam, but you can learn how to conquer it. That's what this book is for. Analyze the reasons for your difficulties to help you decide on a plan of attack.

- Did the unfamiliar format of the questions throw you for a loop? These are unusual questions, unlike what you've probably encountered on standardized exams in the past. You can read more complete descriptions for each part of the test, including the kinds of questions you're likely to encounter, in the chapters that follow.

- Did the short amount of time allowed, particularly for Parts A and C, give you trouble? Practice is the best way to get better at answering these questions quickly. Chapters 5–7 of this book offer you lots of opportunities for practice, and there are also three more complete practice exams in Chapters 9–11.

- Did you do pretty well on some parts and not on others? Maybe you did all right on Parts A and B but really struggled with Part C. Whatever your weakest point, choose that part to work on most diligently in the weeks ahead.

Use this book as much as possible. Familiarity and practice with the kinds of questions given on the exam are the key to your success.

CHAPTER

5 ▶ Address Checking Review

CHAPTER SUMMARY

The ability to work quickly and perform accurately will help you achieve success on Part A of Test 473. This chapter includes hints and strategies to apply on test day as well as 30 sample Address Checking questions for you to practice on.

F or many USPS employees, accuracy in the area of address checking is crucial. If a clerk or carrier misreads an address, the consequences to the customer may cause real misfortune. Efficiency is as important as accuracy. The clerk or carrier must work swiftly so that the mail can go through on time.

This is the reason why Test 473, the Postal Worker Exam, includes a section on checking addresses. At first glance, the Address Checking section would seem to be the easiest part of the exam. However, the time constraint makes it more difficult than it appears on the surface. On the actual exam, you will have only 11 minutes to work on 60 questions. You may not be able to finish them all, but the more you answer correctly, the higher your score will be.

▶ What the Address Checking Section Is Like

In the Address Checking section, you are given two lists, each with two columns. The list on the left is the "Correct List"; everything on this list is as it should be. The two columns in this list are "Address"—these have street numbers, names, cities, and states—and "ZIP Codes"—these have either standard five-digit ZIP codes or nine-digit ZIP codes.

The list on the right is the "List to Be Checked." This list also has a column for addresses and a column for ZIP codes. Your task is to compare all the information in the "List to Be Checked" against all the information in the "Correct List." Here is an example:

	CORRECT LIST		LIST TO BE CHECKED	
QUESTION	ADDRESS	ZIP CODE	ADDRESS	ZIP CODE
1.	1611 Dennis Dr Jonesville, LA	71343-9643	1611 Ennis Dr Jonesville, LA	71343-9643

You may be asking yourself, if this is the question, what are the answer choices? On this part of Test 473, all the Address Checking answer choices are the same. You have to determine whether there are **No errors** (choice **a**), an error in the **Address only** (choice **b**), an error in the **ZIP code only** (choice **c**), or an error in **Both** the address and ZIP code (choice **d**). In the previous example, the answer would be **b**, Address only.

You may not have noticed the slight difference between "Dennis" and "Ennis." The differences between addresses and ZIP codes may be subtle: There may be slight variations in the spellings of cities, towns, or street names, for example, or state and other abbreviations may be similar but not identical. Consider, for example, the differences between Ct and St, between KS and KY, between Schaeffer and Shaeffer, or between 2109 and 2190. Read carefully so that you see what is actually there, not what you expect to see.

Timing and Scoring

It's important to understand both the timing and the scoring on this part of the test. First, you have only 11 minutes to complete as many of the 60 questions as you can. You may not be able to answer all of these questions, just do your best. As you start, aim to answer three questions per minute. On other practice tests, try to improve each time.

If you are running out of time, it is important NOT to fill in bubbles for all the questions you haven't answered. For every incorrect answer, $\frac{1}{3}$ of a point will be deducted from your score. Every point matters when you are trying to pass and get a high placement on the hiring register, so don't lose points for careless errors or guessing.

Part A—Address Checking: A Quick View

SECTION NAME	NUMBER OF QUESTIONS	TIME	SCORING
Part A—Address Checking	60	11 minutes	Guessing penalty of $\frac{1}{3}$ off for each incorrect answer

► Helpful Hints

Here are five hints to keep in mind on test day. They will help you save time, work quickly, and score as many points as you can.

Common Differences

Following are the most common examples of errors you can expect to see:

- Variations in spelling due to missing or added letters

Blair Ferry Rd	Blaire Ferry Rd
Hartford Wy	Harford Wy
Rondell Street	Rondel Street

- Variations in spelling, often with the same pronunciation

Dyersburg	Dyersberg
Hadlyville	Hadleyville
Gare Blvd	Gair Blvd

- Variations in abbreviations

Cir	Ct
WA	MA
St	Dr

- Variations in compass abbreviations

450 NE Warwick Way	450 NW Warwick Way
916 SW Lupe Cir	916 SE Lupe Cir
9637 W Narcisa Ln	9637 Narcisa Ln W

- Transposed numbers in street addresses or ZIP codes

9889 7th St NW	9898 7th St NW
Iowa City, IA 52242	Iowa City, IA 52422
4334 Inocencia Blvd	4343 Inocencia Blvd

- Variations in number of digits

9673	967
34437	3447

- Replacement of one digit by another

63947	63647
4088	4080
9669	9689

Try looking for these variations as you work through the practice materials in this book.

The Choices Never Change

One of the most important things to remember about Address Checking questions is that the answer choices never change. (**Note:** Be sure to check that the answer choices appear in the same order on the official test.) Every question has the same four choices. Before test day, take the time to memorize them so that you don't waste time looking at the answer choices for every question. Here they are again for your review:

- **a.** No errors
- **b.** Address only
- **c.** ZIP code only
- **d.** Both

Keep Your Place

A simple but often overlooked factor that is crucial to your score is to make sure you do not lose your place on the answer sheet. Because of the speed with which you have to work, you can easily skip a number or even a column on the answer sheet and mark a whole series of answers incorrectly before you discover your error. In this portion of the test, seconds count, and you don't want to take the time to erase.

You will not be allowed to use a straight-edge ruler or any other tool on the test itself, so as you work, be sure to use both hands. Hold your pencil in your writing hand and use the index finger of your other hand to run along under the addresses being compared.

Skip a Question If You Want

It is all right to skip, as you may not be able to answer all 60 questions in the 11 minutes. In this part of the test, you will be penalized for wrong answers, so it is not to your advantage to guess or randomly mark your answer sheet. Your score on this part of the test will be based on right answers minus $\frac{1}{3}$ point for wrong answers.

Under the stress of test taking, it's easy to become distracted. So at the beginning, be very careful to pay close attention to the examiner's instructions. Because the abilities being tested are speed and accuracy, the test will be carefully timed. You must not start until you are told to, and you must stop when you are told to. When you are directed to work on a particular part of the exam, work only on that part. If you finish a section before the time is up, you may review your answers, but you may not move on. Failure to follow directions can result in disqualification—and that would be real failure.

Stay Focused

The last hint for Address Checking questions is to stay focused. Losing interest and energy when checking a list of addresses is easy and will cost you valuable minutes. Remember that you will have only 11 minutes to answer 60 questions—that works out to answering six questions every minute. Don't allow yourself to become bored and stop working, even for half a minute. Move quickly from one question to the next, to the extent that you can do so without sacrificing accuracy. Hone your skills using this book so that you will be able to answer as many questions as possible on test day.

► Strategies for Success

Now that you know the hints that will help you do your best on test day, it's time for some of our strategies that will save you time and earn you every point you need to get a top score.

Always Start with the ZIP Code

Even though the ZIP code is the last part of both lists, it is the best place to start for each question. It has the least amount of information. Compared to the address list, which has a street number, name, city, and state, the ZIP code column has five, or at most nine, numbers in it. If you work accurately, it will take less time to compare the two sets of numbers rather than all the address information.

More important though, based on what you find when comparing the two ZIP codes, you can double your chances for finding the correct answer. How does that work?

Well, you have to think of the answer choices. They are:

a. No errors
b. Address only
c. ZIP code only
d. Both

Before you look at either the address or the ZIP code, the answer could be a, b, c, or d. However, if you compare the two ZIP codes and find they are identical, the answer must be a (No errors) or b (Address only). If the ZIP codes are identical, it's impossible for the answer to be c (ZIP code only) or d (Both). It works the same way if you do find an error in the ZIP code. If the two ZIP codes are different, the answer could only be c (ZIP code only) or d (Both). Although you still have to check the address, just by checking the lesser amount of information in the ZIP code columns first, you have doubled your chances of answering correctly.

One Thing at a Time

Once you have checked the ZIP codes and narrowed the answer possibilities, it's time to check the address column. As previously mentioned, these two columns have much more information. Handle all of this information by taking one thing at a time. Begin by comparing the first part of the address on the Correct List (the street number) with the first part of the address on List to Be Checked. Then go back and compare the second part with the second part, the third with the third, and so on. As soon as you see a difference, you can mark your answer based on the difference found in the address column and what you found in the ZIP code column.

Here is an example of just two street addresses to help demonstrate the "one thing at a time" strategy:

36747 Blair Ferry Rd   **37647** Blair Ferry Rd

Start with the first element—the street number, which appears in bold. If you look carefully, you'll quickly see that the number on the left (36747) is different from the number on the right (37647), even though they are very similar. There is no need even to look at the rest of the address since you've established that the two addresses are different. Of course, if the numbers were the same, you should use the same method to continue to compare the street name, city, and state. Because it turns the process of comparing addresses into a system, this strategy helps reduce the likelihood of error.

Read What You See

Another important strategy for avoiding errors is to read what you see. This may sound obvious, but here's what it means. It is natural, when you see the word "Ct" to read it as "Court"; similarly, when you see "Pkwy" you will instinctively think "Parkway." However, it is best to sound out the syllables in your mind, rather than reading complete words: KY should be read "kay-wy," rather than "Kentucky"; 919 should be read "nine-one-nine," rather than "nine-nineteen"; "St" should be read "es-tee," rather than "street," and so on. So, be sure to read what you see, not what you *expect* to see.

▶ Address Checking Review Summary

- Memorize the answer choices, so you don't waste time reading them while answering questions.
- Practice working quickly and accurately. Don't expect to answer all the questions in the time allowed.
- Be sure you do not lose your place on the answer sheet—use both hands.
- Familiarize yourself with the common differences that are likely to appear in the List to Be Checked.
- Always compare the ZIP codes first. They have less information to compare and help you to narrow the answer down to one of two choices.
- After you have checked the ZIP codes, move on to one detail at a time. Compare the two street numbers first, then the street names, then the cities, then the states.
- Read what you see, not what you expect to see— sound the words out silently. (KY is "kay-wy," St is "es-tee," and so on.)
- Do not guess—you will be penalized for wrong answers.
- Skip a question if you want.
- PRACTICE, PRACTICE, PRACTICE.

Following are 30 Address Checking questions, an answer sheet, the questions, and an answer key. To simulate the real test, see how many questions you can answer in six minutes. With practice, your efficiency and accuracy will improve. The practice exams in Chapters 9–11 also feature complete Address Checking questions.

▶ Part A—Address Checking Questions

	a	b	c	d			a	b	c	d			a	b	c	d
1.	ⓐ	ⓑ	ⓒ	ⓓ		11.	ⓐ	ⓑ	ⓒ	ⓓ		21.	ⓐ	ⓑ	ⓒ	ⓓ
2.	ⓐ	ⓑ	ⓒ	ⓓ		12.	ⓐ	ⓑ	ⓒ	ⓓ		22.	ⓐ	ⓑ	ⓒ	ⓓ
3.	ⓐ	ⓑ	ⓒ	ⓓ		13.	ⓐ	ⓑ	ⓒ	ⓓ		23.	ⓐ	ⓑ	ⓒ	ⓓ
4.	ⓐ	ⓑ	ⓒ	ⓓ		14.	ⓐ	ⓑ	ⓒ	ⓓ		24.	ⓐ	ⓑ	ⓒ	ⓓ
5.	ⓐ	ⓑ	ⓒ	ⓓ		15.	ⓐ	ⓑ	ⓒ	ⓓ		25.	ⓐ	ⓑ	ⓒ	ⓓ
6.	ⓐ	ⓑ	ⓒ	ⓓ		16.	ⓐ	ⓑ	ⓒ	ⓓ		26.	ⓐ	ⓑ	ⓒ	ⓓ
7.	ⓐ	ⓑ	ⓒ	ⓓ		17.	ⓐ	ⓑ	ⓒ	ⓓ		27.	ⓐ	ⓑ	ⓒ	ⓓ
8.	ⓐ	ⓑ	ⓒ	ⓓ		18.	ⓐ	ⓑ	ⓒ	ⓓ		28.	ⓐ	ⓑ	ⓒ	ⓓ
9.	ⓐ	ⓑ	ⓒ	ⓓ		19.	ⓐ	ⓑ	ⓒ	ⓓ		29.	ⓐ	ⓑ	ⓒ	ⓓ
10.	ⓐ	ⓑ	ⓒ	ⓓ		20.	ⓐ	ⓑ	ⓒ	ⓓ		30.	ⓐ	ⓑ	ⓒ	ⓓ

Directions: Review and compare the information in the **List to Be Checked** with the information in the **Correct List**. To answer each question, you must decide if there are **No errors (a)**, an error in the **Address only (b)**, an error in the **ZIP code only (c)**, or an error in **Both (d)** the address and the ZIP code.

Time: 6 minutes

	CORRECT LIST		LIST TO BE CHECKED	
QUESTION	ADDRESS	ZIP CODE	ADDRESS	ZIP CODE
1.	4007 Mulberry St Etna, NH	03750	4007 Mulberry St Etna, NH	03750
2.	960 Leheigh Rd Bon Aqua, TN	37025	960 Lehigh Rd Bon Aqua, TN	37025
3.	3290 S Lake Road Hanah, ND	58239	3290 S Lake Road Hanah, ND	58299
4.	881 14th St La Pine, OR	97739	88 14th St La Pine, OR	97379
5.	6771 Southhampton Ct Elm Grove, IL	60443	6771 Southhampton Ct Elm Grove, IL	60443
6.	PO Box 9642 Notus, ID	83656	PO Box 9642 Notus, ID	83665
7.	2039 Westridge Drive Poole, KY	42444-4444	2093 Westridge Drive Poole, KY	42444-4444
8.	33321 Fowler Sedalia, MO	65301	33321 Fowler Sedalia, MO	63501

a. No errors
b. Address only
c. ZIP code only
d. Both

QUESTION	CORRECT LIST		LIST TO BE CHECKED	
	ADDRESS	ZIP CODE	ADDRESS	ZIP CODE
9.	7710 Nilson Blvd Wall, NJ	07719	7710 Nilson Blvd Wall, NY	07119
10.	4337 Nguyen Wy West Bath, ME	04530	4337 Nguyen Wy West Bath, ME	04530
11.	916 McMurray Ct Petty, TX	75470	916 McMurray Ct Petty, TX	75070
12.	3030 Prairie Rd Floyd, NM	88118	3030 Prairie Dr Floyd, NM	88118
13.	4370 McCollogh Way Byram, MS	39272-2366	4370 McCollogh Way Bryam, MO	39272-2366
14.	9008 Schaeffer St Crete, NE	68333	9008 Schaeffer St Crete, NM	68333
15.	210 Pittman Rd Beaman, IA	50609	210 Pittmann Rd Beaman, IA	56009
16.	961 Old Post Hwy Cub Run, KY	42729	961 Old Post Hwy Cub Run, KY	42729
17.	997 Woodcrest Dr Fine, NY	13639-7089	997 Woodcrest Dr Fino, NY	13639-7098
18.	1717 Stevens Ct Hamlin, WV	25523	1717 Steven Ct Hamlin, WV	25223
19.	26 Naaktgeboren St Hachita, NM	88040	26 Naaktgeboren St Hachita, NM	88040
20.	9969 Western Blvd Gusher, UT	84026	9969 Western Blvd Usher, UT	84026
21.	419 Dunsbar Halleck, NV	89824	419 Dunbar Halleck, NV	89924
22.	9401 Steindler Blvd Mauk, GA	31058-0013	9401 Steindler Blvd Mauk, GA	31058-0013

a. No errors
b. Address only
c. ZIP code only
d. Both

	CORRECT LIST		LIST TO BE CHECKED	
QUESTION	ADDRESS	ZIP CODE	ADDRESS	ZIP CODE
23.	4112 Mont St Pana, IL	62557	4112 Mont St Pana, IL	62257
24.	9667 Ferndale Ln Santa Barbara, CA	93160	9676 Ferndale Ln Santa Barbara, CA	93160
25.	4647 Chaloupek Sparks, MD	21152	4648 Chaloupek Sparks, MD	21152
26.	7614 Brown Deer Rd Van Meter, PA	15479-4575	7614 Brown Deer Rd Van Meter, PA	15479-4755
27.	437 Mt Veeder Rd Pachuta, MS	39347	437 Mt Veeder Dr Pachuta, MS	33347
28.	9772 Sharon Center Rd Eaton, CO	80615	9772 Sharon Center Rd Eaton, CO	86015
29.	79 McGee St Alix, AR	72820-3346	79 McGee St Alix, AK	72820-3346
30.	4969 Myers Blvd Ferney, SD	57439	4699 Myers Blvd Ferney, SD	57439

a. No errors
b. Address only
c. ZIP code only
d. Both

► Answers

1. a.	**11.** c.	**21.** d.
2. b.	**12.** b.	**22.** a.
3. c.	**13.** b.	**23.** c.
4. d.	**14.** b.	**24.** b.
5. a.	**15.** d.	**25.** b.
6. c.	**16.** a.	**26.** c.
7. b.	**17.** d.	**27.** d.
8. c.	**18.** d.	**28.** c.
9. d.	**19.** a.	**29.** b.
10. a.	**20.** b.	**30.** b.

6 ▶ Forms Completion Review

CHAPTER SUMMARY

Paying attention to detail is critical to getting a top score on Part B of Test 473, the Postal Worker Exam. This chapter includes hints and strategies to apply on test day as well as 15 sample Forms Completion questions for you to practice on.

ike any large business, the USPS relies heavily on forms for processing, tracking, and filing its services and the billions of pieces of mail it handles every year. However, a form is useful only if it is filled out completely *and* accurately. This is the reason why Test 473 includes a section on completing forms. While this probably is the easiest part of the test, it still requires some preparation and practice on your part. You will have only 15 minutes to review the forms and answer 30 multiple-choice questions. To get a good score, it is important that you answer every question as best you can. Keep reading to learn more.

▶ What the Forms Completion Section Is Like

In the Forms Completion section, you are shown a sample form, such as one that would be used by the USPS. Some examples include a "Change of Address" form, a form to hold mail, or a customs form. Each form is followed by seven to ten questions, for a total of 30 questions in this part of the exam. Here is an example of a basic form:

Sample Form

1. Last Name	
1A. First Name	
2. Address	
2A. City	
2B. State	2C. ZIP Code
3. Signature	
3A. Date	4. Postmark

The forms you will see on test day will vary, but you can expect to see forms with several boxes and lines that need to be filled in. However, your task on this part of the test is not to fill in the form. Instead, you will be answering multiple-choice questions about the forms. A sample question for this form might be:

1. Which of the following would complete box 2B?
   a. address
   b. city
   c. state
   d. ZIP code

The answer, of course, is **c**. The key is to use the information found on the forms to answer the questions.

Timing and Scoring

On this part of the exam, you have 15 minutes to complete 30 questions. You should try to pace yourself so that you are answering one question every 25 seconds. However, if you are running out of time, you should always fill in bubbles for all the questions you haven't answered yet. Remember, there is no guessing penalty on this part of the test, so it is to your advantage to guess on any questions you haven't had time to answer.

▶ Helpful Hints

Here are several hints to keep in mind on test day. They will help you save time, work quickly, and score as many points as you can.

Know the Question Types

The more you know about an exam before you take it, the less likely you are to panic when you encounter each new part. Because Part B has a variety of question types, it's helpful to review them before test day. Here are a few of the question types you might see.

SECTION NAME	NUMBER OF QUESTIONS	TIME	SCORING
Part B—Forms Completion	30	15 minutes	No guessing penalty

In which box does the information belong?

Example

Which box would contain a ZIP code?

a. 1

b. 2

c. 3

d. 4

What information belongs in a certain box?

Example

Box 3a contains which of the following?

a. description of merchandise

b. last name

c. check mark

d. fees

How much information is found on the form?

Example

How many dates are required for this receipt?

a. 0

b. 1

c. 2

d. 3

There are other examples, so be sure to pay attention as you complete the practice questions in this chapter and the practice exams in this book.

Keep Pace and Keep Your Place

As always, you should make sure you do not lose your place on the answer sheet. Even though you have roughly 30 seconds to answer each question, you can easily skip a number or even a column on the answer sheet and mark a whole series of answers incorrectly before you discover your error.

► Strategies for Success

Now it's time for some of the strategies that will help you earn maximum points on this section.

Form First, Questions Second

All of the questions in this part of the exam are based on forms, so it should make sense to review the forms first. Before you answer any questions, take at least 30 seconds, but no more than 90, to study the form and its contents. If you are already familiar with the form when you start to answer questions, you will be able to answer them more quickly and accurately. Also, be sure to read the questions carefully so that you understand exactly what they are asking.

Review All Answer Choices

Remember that in Parts A and C, all the answer choices are the same. In Part B, however, the answer choices are different for each and every question. For this reason, you should always be careful to review the answer choices before you decide on the answer. Even if you think you are certain of the answer, read each choice carefully.

Guess!

There is NO guessing penalty on Part B of Test 473. For this reason, if you are running out of time and haven't finished the 30 questions, fill in bubbles for all remaining questions. You might even get a few extra points as a result of pure luck. As always, every point matters when you are trying to pass and get a high placement on the hiring register, so take advantage of the opportunity to guess without a penalty if you are running out of time.

Never Answer from Memory

The final strategy refers back to the first. Never forget that the questions are based on the form. Even if you are on the last question and you are certain you have memorized the form and know the answer, refer back to it, just in case. If you figure that all the answers are found right there on the test, you should always take an extra few seconds to confirm that your choice is correct.

▶ Forms Completion Review Summary

- Review the question types so you know what to expect on test day.
- Be sure you do not lose your place on the answer sheet.
- Always study the form before you start answering the questions. Spend at least 30 seconds reviewing the form and then be sure to read the questions carefully.
- Know that answer choices on this part of the test are different for each question, and read all answer choices before selecting the answer.
- Never answer a question from memory; always refer back to the form to confirm the answer.
- If you are running out of time, guess! There is no penalty for wrong answers.
- PRACTICE, PRACTICE, PRACTICE.

What follows are 15 Forms Completion questions, an answer sheet, and an answer key. To simulate the real test, give yourself only eight minutes to complete these questions. The practice exams in Chapters 9–11 also feature complete Forms Completion sections.

Directions: Review each form and answer the questions that follow.

Time: 8 minutes

▶ Practice Forms Completion Questions

1.	ⓐ	ⓑ	ⓒ	ⓓ	6.	ⓐ	ⓑ	ⓒ	ⓓ	11.	ⓐ	ⓑ	ⓒ	ⓓ
2.	ⓐ	ⓑ	ⓒ	ⓓ	7.	ⓐ	ⓑ	ⓒ	ⓓ	12.	ⓐ	ⓑ	ⓒ	ⓓ
3.	ⓐ	ⓑ	ⓒ	ⓓ	8.	ⓐ	ⓑ	ⓒ	ⓓ	13.	ⓐ	ⓑ	ⓒ	ⓓ
4.	ⓐ	ⓑ	ⓒ	ⓓ	9.	ⓐ	ⓑ	ⓒ	ⓓ	14.	ⓐ	ⓑ	ⓒ	ⓓ
5.	ⓐ	ⓑ	ⓒ	ⓓ	10.	ⓐ	ⓑ	ⓒ	ⓓ	15.	ⓐ	ⓑ	ⓒ	ⓓ

Attempt to Deliver Notifications

1. Delivery Attempt 1 (a) Mo. (b) Day	2. Time [ ] a. _____ AM [ ] b. _____ PM	7. Carrier's Signature
3. Next Delivery Attempt to be made on (a) Mo. (b) Day	4. Time [ ] a. _____ AM [ ] b. _____ PM	7A. Carrier's ID Number
5. Final Attempt (a) Mo. (b) Day	6. Time [ ] a. _____ AM [ ] b. _____ PM	8. Postmark

1. Which of the following would complete box 7?
   a. signature
   b. ID number
   c. postmark
   d. stamp

2. If the first delivery attempt is made at four in the afternoon, which box would be checked?
   a. 2b
   b. 4b
   c. 6b
   d. 7b

3. A postmark would complete which of the following?
   a. box 7
   b. box 7A
   c. box 7B
   d. box 8

4. If the next attempt is going to be made on 4/24/09, what would belong in line 3a?
   a. 24
   b. 2009
   c. April
   d. 4/24/09

5. How many days would complete this form?
   a. 1
   b. 2
   c. 3
   d. 4

6. If an ID number is "98630," where would it belong?
   a. 2a
   b. 4b
   c. 7
   d. 7A

7. Where should the carrier sign?
   a. box 6
   b. box 7
   c. box 7A
   d. box 8

Signature Confirmed Receipt

1. Last Name	1A. First Name
1B. Address	
1C. City	1D. State
1E. ZIP	1F. +4 ZIP

2. Right to Waive Signature

a. [　] Yes　If "yes" sign at　　　　　　　　b. [　] No　If "no" proceed to box 4

3. Signature

3a. Date

4. Item Sent

(a) letter [　]　　　　(b) magazine [　]　　　　(c) box [　]　　　　(d) other [　]

---

8. Where does the ZIP code belong?
- **a.** box 1C
- **b.** box 1D
- **c.** box 1E
- **d.** box 1F

9. Which of the following would complete box 4?
- **a.** postmark
- **b.** check mark
- **c.** date
- **d.** signature

10. The first name belongs in which of the following?
- **a.** box 1
- **b.** box 1A
- **c.** box 2
- **d.** box 3a

11. Which of the following is an appropriate entry for box 1D?
- **a.** 30 W 10th Street
- **b.** Tucson
- **c.** AZ
- **d.** 85726

12. Where does the date belong on this form?
- **a.** box 3
- **b.** box 3a
- **c.** box 4a
- **d.** box 4b

13. "Des Moines" would be an appropriate entry for which box?
- **a.** 1B
- **b.** 1C
- **c.** 1D
- **d.** 1E

14. Signing the form is NOT required if there is a check mark in which box?
- **a.** 2a
- **b.** 2b
- **c.** 3
- **d.** 3a

15. If the item being sent is a magazine, which box would include a check mark?
- **a.** 4b
- **b.** 4c
- **c.** 4d
- **d.** 4e

▶ **Answers**

1. b. Box 7 would be completed by the carrier's signature.

2. a. The first delivery attempt time is identified in box 2a or 2b. Because the delivery was made in the afternoon, the P.M. box, 2b, would be checked.

3. d. The postmark belongs in box 8.

4. c. Line 3a requires the month, April.

5. c. The day of the first delivery, the next attempt, and the final attempt are all listed; therefore, 3 is the correct answer.

6. d. The carrier's ID number belongs in box 7A.

7. b. The carrier's signature belongs in box 7.

8. c. The ZIP code belongs in box 1E.

9. a. Box 4 requires a check mark.

10. b. The first name belongs in box 1A.

11. c. A state (AZ) belongs in box 1D.

12. b. The date belongs in box 3a.

13. b. Des Moines is a city, so it belongs in box 1C.

14. b. If box 2b is checked, the instructions read "proceed to box 4." Therefore, the signature is not required.

15. a. According to the form, a check mark in box 4b would mean a magazine is being sent.

Coding and Memory Review

CHAPTER SUMMARY

Working quickly and having a strong memory are critical to succeeding on both sections of Part C of Test 473. This chapter will review both the Coding and Memory questions as well as the hints and strategies for doing your best. You will also find 36 practice questions to improve your coding and memory skills.

Every year, the USPS delivers hundreds of billions of pieces of mail to more than 142 million businesses, residences, and P.O. boxes. How does all of this mail get sorted and delivered? Very quickly and very carefully, of course. To achieve this, USPS employees need to be able to code every piece of mail for its delivery route. For this reason, Part C of the Postal Worker Exam uses two sections to test potential employees in coding and memory skills.

Part C also tests your speed. There are 36 questions on each section (72 questions altogether), but there is only a total of 13 minutes to answer as many questions as you can. Fortunately, you are not expected to answer every question, but you should make every attempt to earn as many points as possible.

▶ About the Coding Section

The Coding section begins with a Coding Guide, such as the one that follows. This guide shows four delivery routes: A, B, C, and D. For delivery routes A, B, and C, address ranges are given. Any addresses not belonging to one of those ranges is directed to delivery route D. Your task is to look at the address in each question and determine to which delivery route it belongs. Here is a sample question that would follow the Coding Guide:

CODING GUIDE	
ADDRESS RANGE	**DELIVERY ROUTE**
50–300 Up Ave 1–20 Down Street	A
700–1550 Here Blvd 600–1200 Somewhere Lane 10–80 N There Street	B
81–120 N There Street 1700–2200 Here Blvd 1201–1700 Somewhere Lane	C
All mail that doesn't belong in one of the address ranges listed here.	D

1. 55 Up Ave
   a. Delivery Route A
   b. Delivery Route B
   c. Delivery Route C
   d. Delivery Route D

The correct answer is **a**; 55 falls within the range of 50–300 Up Ave., so it belongs in delivery route A.

Although these questions seem straightforward, the limited time can make this section a real challenge. You need to stay on task and focused in order to succeed. Now let's review the Memory section of Part C.

▶ About the Memory Section

The difference between Coding questions and Memory questions is this: While answering Coding questions, you are able to refer back to the Coding Guide as often

as needed. In the Memory section, the *exact same* Coding Guide is given, but you are given only three minutes to memorize it.

The questions are the same type as in the Coding section (you are given an address and must determine to which delivery route it belongs), but in addition to being tested on your speed, you will also be tested on your memory. During the three-minute study period, you are NOT allowed to take notes and you are never allowed to turn your test book back to the Coding Guide once the study time is over. Your task is to memorize the chart as best you can and to answer as many questions as you can.

Timing and Scoring on Both Sections

The timing is slightly different for each section of Part C. You will have six minutes to answer as many of the 36 Coding questions as you can. For the Memory questions,

More about the Coding Guide

The Coding Guide has three sets of two street address ranges and two separate street address ranges. For example, in the sample Coding Guide in this chapter, there are two ranges for Here Blvd., two ranges for There Street, and two ranges of Somewhere Lane. There is also one range for Up Ave. and one range for Down Street. On occasion, the number of address ranges will vary by box. For example, there may be two address ranges in box A and three each in boxes B and C. Other Coding Guides may have three address ranges in boxes A and C, while box B has only two. Knowing these facts about the Coding Guide will help when you have to memorize it.

SECTION NAME	NUMBER OF QUESTIONS	TIME	SCORING
Part C, Section 1—Coding	36	6 minutes	Guessing penalty of $\frac{1}{3}$ off for each incorrect answer
Part C, Section 2—Memory	36	3 minutes for memorization, 7 minutes to answer questions	Guessing penalty of $\frac{1}{3}$ off for each incorrect answer

you will first have three minutes to memorize the Coding Guide. Then, you will have seven minutes to answer as many of the 36 Memory questions as you can.

If you are running out of time, it is important NOT to fill in bubbles for all the questions you haven't answered. For every incorrect answer, $\frac{1}{3}$ of a point will be deducted from your score. Every point matters when you are trying to pass and get a high placement on the hiring register, so don't lose points for careless errors or guessing.

▶ Helpful Hints

Here are some hints for test day. They will help you save time, work quickly, and score as many points as you can.

Delivery Route D Differences

It is important to keep in mind that there are three major differences to indicate that the answer to a question is Delivery Route D. Here is the sample Coding Guide and the differences some questions show:

CODING GUIDE	
ADDRESS RANGE	**DELIVERY ROUTE**
50–300 Up Ave 1–20 Down Street	A
700–1550 Here Blvd 600–1200 Somewhere Lane 10–80 N There Street	B
81–120 N There Street 1700–2200 Here Blvd 1201–1700 Somewhere Lane	C
All mail that doesn't belong in one of the address ranges listed here.	D

- **Difference in Number.** These questions show an address number that is not included within the ranges listed for routes A, B, or C. For example, 49 Up Ave. is below the range shown for route A; therefore, it belongs in route D.

- **Difference in Street Name.** These questions show a street name that is different (sometimes only in spelling) than the streets listed for routes A, B, or C. For example, 17 Downing Street is different from 17 Down Street; therefore, it belongs in route D.

Always be very careful to pay close attention to the examiner's instructions. The study period during the Memory section is strictly regulated. You must NOT take notes, and you are not allowed to refer back to the Coding Guide once you have started answering Memory questions. Either of these actions is likely to result in your immediate failure of Test 473.

■ **Difference in Street Type.** These questions show a street type (street, avenue, boulevard, way, circle, drive, road, etc.) that is different from the street type already associated with one of the streets. For example, 1201 Somewhere Drive is different from 1201 Somewhere Lane; therefore, it belongs in route D.

Try looking for these differences as you work through the practice questions in this book.

The Choices Never Change

One of the most important things to remember about Coding and Memory questions is that the answer choices never change. Every question has the same four choices. Before test day, take the time to memorize them so that you don't waste time looking at the answer choices for every question. Here they are again for your review:

    a. Delivery Route A
    b. Delivery Route B
    c. Delivery Route C
    d. Delivery Route D

Keep Your Place

One factor that is crucial to your score is to make sure you do not lose your place on the answer sheet. Because of the speed with which you have to work, you can easily skip a number or even a column on the answer sheet and mark a whole series of answers incorrectly before you discover your error. In this portion of the test, every second counts, and you don't want to have to take time to erase and start again.

Skip a Question If You Want

It is all right to skip around within a section, as you are not expected to answer all of the questions in the time allotted. In both sections of Part C, you will be penalized for wrong answers, so it is NOT to your advantage to guess or just randomly mark your answer sheet. Your score on this part of the test will be based on right answers minus $\frac{1}{3}$ point for wrong answers.

Stay Focused

Losing interest and energy on the Coding section and forgetting the Coding Guide on the Memory section is easy and will cost you valuable time and points. In the Coding section, don't allow yourself to become bored and stop working, even for half a minute. Move quickly from one question to the next, but try to maintain your accuracy. If you do draw a blank on the Memory section, stop, take a mental break for no more than ten seconds, and collect your memory of the Coding Guide. Don't give up.

▶ Strategies for Success

Here are some strategies that will help you earn as many points as possible on test day.

Start Memorizing During the Coding Section

One of the most helpful parts of the Coding and Memory sections is that the Coding Guide is *exactly the same* for both sections. This means that even before the study period in the Memory section, you will have already had some time to review the Coding Guide.

Simplifying Street Numbers—Pros and Cons

Let's look at the address ranges from the Coding Guide already used in this chapter:

CODING GUIDE
ADDRESS RANGE
50–300 Up Ave
1–20 Down Street
700–1550 Here Blvd
600–1200 Somewhere Lane
10–80 N There Street
81–120 N There Street
1700–2200 Here Blvd
1201–1700 Somewhere Lane

When memorizing the Coding Guide, it is possible to "shorten" some of the address ranges. For example, You can take a shortcut when studying by cutting 600–1200 or 1700–2200 down to 6–12 or 17–22. However, you do need to remember the original numbers that the shortcuts represent so you don't mistake 17000 for 1700 when selecting the delivery route.

During the Coding section, you should answer questions and familiarize yourself as much as you can with the Coding Guide. Don't stop answering Coding questions to memorize the guide, but start by seeing if you can remember at least one of the boxes in it.

Use the Process of Elimination

If you remember from Chapter 3, The LearningExpress Test Preparation System, the process of elimination helps you narrow down your choices to find the correct answer. Because the Coding Guide is so detailed, if you can eliminate even one of the choices, you will have already improved your chances of guessing correctly by 25%!

Ignore Box D

Although there are four delivery routes, you shouldn't spend any time worrying about box D. If you think

about it, you really have to memorize only three boxes (A, B, and C). Anything that doesn't belong in those three boxes automatically is coded to route D. If you've spent enough time memorizing boxes A, B, and C, then you should never have to think about box D.

Memorize Street Names and Boxes First

Unfortunately, because of how the Coding Guide and questions are written, the best way to succeed on these sections is simply to memorize the information in boxes A, B, and C. To be more specific, we suggest memorizing the street names and corresponding routes first. When you get started, pretend the numbers aren't there. Simplified by taking away the numbers and ignoring box D, the Coding Guide would look like this:

CODING GUIDE	
ADDRESS RANGE	**DELIVERY ROUTE**
Up Ave.	A
Down Street	
Here Blvd.	B
Somewhere Lane	
N There Street	
N There Street	C
Here Blvd.	
Somewhere Lane	

Although this method will not allow you to answer many questions correctly, at a minimum you will be able to eliminate at least one incorrect choice. For example, if you are given 1456 Somewhere Lane, you at least know for certain that the answer is NOT **a**. You would have to know the ranges to answer the question, but if you are drawing a blank, this is a start toward answering questions correctly.

Make Notes *after* the Study Period

Taking notes is strictly forbidden during the study period. However, as soon as you are told to begin answering the Memory questions, you are able to write in the test book. If you want to make notes from your

Simplifying Street Names—Pros and Cons

Let's take another look at the sample Coding Guide already used in this chapter:

CODING GUIDE	
ADDRESS RANGE	**DELIVERY ROUTE**
50–300 Up Ave	A
1–20 Down Street	
700–1550 Here Blvd	B
600–1200 Somewhere Lane	
10–80 N There Street	
81–120 N There Street	C
1700–2200 Here Blvd	
1201–1700 Somewhere Lane	
All mail that doesn't belong in one of the address ranges listed here.	D

This strategy suggests that instead of memorizing the full name of every street, simplify them to two syllables. For example, you don't have to memorize **So**mewhere **La**ne, instead, memorize **SoLa**. The less you have to remember, the less you have to forget. However, and this is **very important**, let's say you come across a question of 675 Southern Lane. Based on your abbreviation of SoLa, you might think the answer is **b**. You would be wrong; 675 Southern Lane is not the same as 675 Somewhere Lane and you would have just cost yourself $\frac{1}{3}$ of a point. Abbreviations are helpful when memorizing so many names, but know what the abbreviation actually stands for.

memory of the Coding Guide, this is your chance, since you are not allowed to refer back to it at any time. Do not be tempted to make any notes at all during the study period; you must wait until the questions have begun.

▶ Coding and Memory Review Summary

- Familiarize yourself with the differences that would make an address belong in Route D: difference in address range, street name, or street type.
- Memorize the answer choices, so you don't waste time reading them while answering questions.
- Skip questions in a section and move on to others you might be more certain of because you will not be able to answer all the questions in the time allowed.
- Stay focused and be sure you do not lose your place on the answer sheet.
- Start memorizing the Coding Guide during the Coding section. Remember, it's the exact same guide that is used in the Memory section.

- Use the process of elimination to avoid clearly incorrect answers when you are uncertain. However, do not simply guess randomly—you will be penalized for wrong answers.
- Ignore box D. There is nothing there you need to memorize.
- On the Memory section, memorize the street names and their corresponding boxes first. This will help you during the process of elimination.
- Use memory tricks like simplifying street numbers and street names when possible, but don't forget what your abbreviations represent.
- After the study period, make notes from your memory of the Coding Guide.
- PRACTICE, PRACTICE, PRACTICE.

The best way to prepare for Part C of Test 473 is to practice. Here are 36 Coding and Memory questions for this purpose. There is an answer sheet, the questions, and an answer key. To simulate the real test, give yourself only three minutes to complete the Coding questions, only 90 seconds to memorize the Coding Guide, and finally, three minutes to answer the Memory questions. With practice, your speed and efficiency will improve. The practice exams in Chapters 9–11 also feature complete Coding and Memory sections.

▶ Practice Coding and Memory Questions

Section 1—Coding

1.	ⓐ	ⓑ	ⓒ	ⓓ	7.	ⓐ	ⓑ	ⓒ	ⓓ	13.	ⓐ	ⓑ	ⓒ	ⓓ
2.	ⓐ	ⓑ	ⓒ	ⓓ	8.	ⓐ	ⓑ	ⓒ	ⓓ	14.	ⓐ	ⓑ	ⓒ	ⓓ
3.	ⓐ	ⓑ	ⓒ	ⓓ	9.	ⓐ	ⓑ	ⓒ	ⓓ	15.	ⓐ	ⓑ	ⓒ	ⓓ
4.	ⓐ	ⓑ	ⓒ	ⓓ	10.	ⓐ	ⓑ	ⓒ	ⓓ	16.	ⓐ	ⓑ	ⓒ	ⓓ
5.	ⓐ	ⓑ	ⓒ	ⓓ	11.	ⓐ	ⓑ	ⓒ	ⓓ	17.	ⓐ	ⓑ	ⓒ	ⓓ
6.	ⓐ	ⓑ	ⓒ	ⓓ	12.	ⓐ	ⓑ	ⓒ	ⓓ	18.	ⓐ	ⓑ	ⓒ	ⓓ

Section 2—Memory

19.	ⓐ	ⓑ	ⓒ	ⓓ	25.	ⓐ	ⓑ	ⓒ	ⓓ	31.	ⓐ	ⓑ	ⓒ	ⓓ
20.	ⓐ	ⓑ	ⓒ	ⓓ	26.	ⓐ	ⓑ	ⓒ	ⓓ	32.	ⓐ	ⓑ	ⓒ	ⓓ
21.	ⓐ	ⓑ	ⓒ	ⓓ	27.	ⓐ	ⓑ	ⓒ	ⓓ	33.	ⓐ	ⓑ	ⓒ	ⓓ
22.	ⓐ	ⓑ	ⓒ	ⓓ	28.	ⓐ	ⓑ	ⓒ	ⓓ	34.	ⓐ	ⓑ	ⓒ	ⓓ
23.	ⓐ	ⓑ	ⓒ	ⓓ	29.	ⓐ	ⓑ	ⓒ	ⓓ	35.	ⓐ	ⓑ	ⓒ	ⓓ
24.	ⓐ	ⓑ	ⓒ	ⓓ	30.	ⓐ	ⓑ	ⓒ	ⓓ	36.	ⓐ	ⓑ	ⓒ	ⓓ

Section 1—Coding

Directions: Read and review the **Coding Guide**. Each question offers an **Address**. Choose which **Delivery Route** each address belongs in according to the Coding Guide.

Time: 3 minutes

CODING GUIDE	
ADDRESS RANGE ROUTE	**DELIVER**
801–1600 Lawson Way 200–1500 Curran Lane 300–1700 11th Ave	A
11000–17000 Billett Street 1–99 Notting Drive	B
1701–2300 11th Ave 19000–21000 Billett Street 100–1199 Notting Drive	C
All mail that doesn't belong in one of the address ranges listed here.	D

1. 250 Curran Lane
   a. Delivery Route A
   b. Delivery Route B
   c. Delivery Route C
   d. Delivery Route D

2. 2222 11th Ave
   a. Delivery Route A
   b. Delivery Route B
   c. Delivery Route C
   d. Delivery Route D

3. 12345 Billett Street
   a. Delivery Route A
   b. Delivery Route B
   c. Delivery Route C
   d. Delivery Route D

4. 801 Lawson Drive
   a. Delivery Route A
   b. Delivery Route B
   c. Delivery Route C
   d. Delivery Route D

5. 117 Curran Lane
   a. Delivery Route A
   b. Delivery Route B
   c. Delivery Route C
   d. Delivery Route D

6. 16453 Billett Street
   a. Delivery Route A
   b. Delivery Route B
   c. Delivery Route C
   d. Delivery Route D

7. 1199 Notting Hill Drive
   a. Delivery Route A
   b. Delivery Route B
   c. Delivery Route C
   d. Delivery Route D

8. 20001 Billett Street
   a. Delivery Route A
   b. Delivery Route B
   c. Delivery Route C
   d. Delivery Route D

9. 1470 Curran Lane
   a. Delivery Route A
   b. Delivery Route B
   c. Delivery Route C
   d. Delivery Route D

10. 73 Notting Drive
   a. Delivery Route A
   b. Delivery Route B
   c. Delivery Route C
   d. Delivery Route D

11. 2567 11th Ave
   a. Delivery Route A
   b. Delivery Route B
   c. Delivery Route C
   d. Delivery Route D

12. 11 Notting Drive
   a. Delivery Route A
   b. Delivery Route B
   c. Delivery Route C
   d. Delivery Route D

13. 1489 Curman Lane
   a. Delivery Route A
   b. Delivery Route B
   c. Delivery Route C
   d. Delivery Route D

14. 411 11th Ave
   a. Delivery Route A
   b. Delivery Route B
   c. Delivery Route C
   d. Delivery Route D

15. 894 Notting Drive
   a. Delivery Route A
   b. Delivery Route B
   c. Delivery Route C
   d. Delivery Route D

16. 16999 Billett Street
   a. Delivery Route A
   b. Delivery Route B
   c. Delivery Route C
   d. Delivery Route D

17. 1700 11th St
   a. Delivery Route A
   b. Delivery Route B
   c. Delivery Route C
   d. Delivery Route D

18. 1600 Lawson Way
   a. Delivery Route A
   b. Delivery Route B
   c. Delivery Route C
   d. Delivery Route D

Section 2—Memory

Directions: Spend 90 seconds memorizing the information found in the **Coding Guide**. You may NOT take any notes during this time. Next, you will answer the questions. Each question offers an **Address**. Choose which **Delivery Route** each address belongs in according to your memory of the Coding Guide. **Note: You may NOT turn back to the page displaying the Coding Guide.**

Time: 90 seconds for memorization, 4 minutes to answer questions

CODING GUIDE	
ADDRESS RANGE	**DELIVERY ROUTE**
801–1600 Lawson Way 200–1500 Curran Lane 300–1700 11th Ave	A
11000–17000 Billett Street 1–99 Notting Drive	B
1701–2300 11th Ave 19000–21000 Billett Street 100–1199 Notting Drive	C
All mail that doesn't belong in one of the address ranges listed here.	D

19. 12342 Lewis Street
  a. Delivery Route A
  b. Delivery Route B
  c. Delivery Route C
  d. Delivery Route D

20. 1798 11th Ave
  a. Delivery Route A
  b. Delivery Route B
  c. Delivery Route C
  d. Delivery Route D

21. 676 Curran Lane
  a. Delivery Route A
  b. Delivery Route B
  c. Delivery Route C
  d. Delivery Route D

22. 1139 Nothing Drive
  a. Delivery Route A
  b. Delivery Route B
  c. Delivery Route C
  d. Delivery Route D

23. 100 Notting Drive
  a. Delivery Route A
  b. Delivery Route B
  c. Delivery Route C
  d. Delivery Route D

24. 1998 Curran Lane
  a. Delivery Route A
  b. Delivery Route B
  c. Delivery Route C
  d. Delivery Route D

25. 304 11th Ave
  a. Delivery Route A
  b. Delivery Route B
  c. Delivery Route C
  d. Delivery Route D

26. 19876 Billett Street
  a. Delivery Route A
  b. Delivery Route B
  c. Delivery Route C
  d. Delivery Route D

27. 655 Notting Way
  a. Delivery Route A
  b. Delivery Route B
  c. Delivery Route C
  d. Delivery Route D

28. 15342 Billett Street
  a. Delivery Route A
  b. Delivery Route B
  c. Delivery Route C
  d. Delivery Route D

29. 1432 Curran Lane
  a. Delivery Route A
  b. Delivery Route B
  c. Delivery Route C
  d. Delivery Route D

30. 2295 11th Ave
  a. Delivery Route A
  b. Delivery Route B
  c. Delivery Route C
  d. Delivery Route D

31. 18755 Billett Road
  a. Delivery Route A
  b. Delivery Route B
  c. Delivery Route C
  d. Delivery Route D

32. 14 Notting Drive
  a. Delivery Route A
  b. Delivery Route B
  c. Delivery Route C
  d. Delivery Route D

33. 1343 11th Ave
   a. Delivery Route A
   b. Delivery Route B
   c. Delivery Route C
   d. Delivery Route D

34. 454 Notting Drive
   a. Delivery Route A
   b. Delivery Route B
   c. Delivery Route C
   d. Delivery Route D

35. 76 Notting Drive
   a. Delivery Route A
   b. Delivery Route B
   c. Delivery Route C
   d. Delivery Route D

36. 1700 Lawson Way
   a. Delivery Route A
   b. Delivery Route B
   c. Delivery Route C
   d. Delivery Route D

► Answers

Coding	Memory
1. a.	**19.** d.
2. c.	**20.** c.
3. b.	**21.** a.
4. d.	**22.** d.
5. d.	**23.** c.
6. b.	**24.** d.
7. d.	**25.** a.
8. c.	**26.** c.
9. a.	**27.** d.
10. b.	**28.** b.
11. d.	**29.** a.
12. b.	**30.** c.
13. d.	**31.** d.
14. a.	**32.** b.
15. c.	**33.** a.
16. b.	**34.** c.
17. d.	**35.** b.
18. a.	**36.** d.

8 ▶ Personal Characteristics and Experience Inventory Review and Questions

CHAPTER SUMMARY

Unlike the rest of the test, Part D does not measure any kind of cognitive skill. Nor do the items on this section, strictly speaking, have right or wrong answers. It measures personality or character, not knowledge or skills. Unfortunately, the USPS does not disclose either what personal characteristics its test measures, or how the results are scored. Based on similar tests used by other major employers, we can say that the test most likely measures some of the following:

- personality traits that affect how people act in various types of situations—for example, how outgoing or sociable you are
- interests that influence how you prefer to spend your time—for example, how much you like working with tools or machinery
- ways of thinking, or types of behavior, that would be expected to interfere badly with successful performance on the job
- experiential preferences that may indicate the best person-position fit

When taking this kind of test, the general rule is to be honest and forthcoming; don't try to make yourself look like what the employer wants. There are several reasons for this. First, you do not know exactly what the employer wants. Second, you do not know exactly how the test is scored. (Probably your answers are being compared to those given by other test takers—but how did they respond?) Third, and most important, these tests often include items designed to identify people who are trying to make themselves appear different from what they are; this will influence the interpretation of your scores on other parts of the exam.

Your exam may even be completely discarded. If, for example, you see a statement that sounds "too good to be true," it probably is. Do not try to second-guess the test, either. It was written by professionals who are experts in trapping people who try to do this.

You can do very little to prepare for the test; however, it is important. People can do well on the first three sections of the examination and still be considered unsuitable for hire due to the things they say about themselves on the Personal Characteristics and Experiences Inventory—Part D. Some people may have characteristics that would be problematic in a certain work setting; others may have characteristics that are perfectly desirable, but are not right for a particular job. So, tests like this can aid in helping to match people with the right job—one in which they will be happy and successful. This is another reason to be honest.

Try taking the abbreviated Personal Characteristics and Experience Inventory on the next few pages. Choose only one answer for each question. Then, score your own test and read about what it measures. (The actual test has 236 items. You are allowed 90 minutes in which to complete it, but most people finish sooner. This shorter test will probably take only 20 minutes or so.)

▶ Section 1

1.	(a)	(b)	(c)	(d)	8.	(a)	(b)	(c)	(d)	15.	(a)	(b)	(c)	(d)
2.	(a)	(b)	(c)	(d)	9.	(a)	(b)	(c)	(d)	16.	(a)	(b)	(c)	(d)
3.	(a)	(b)	(c)	(d)	10.	(a)	(b)	(c)	(d)	17.	(a)	(b)	(c)	(d)
4.	(a)	(b)	(c)	(d)	11.	(a)	(b)	(c)	(d)	18.	(a)	(b)	(c)	(d)
5.	(a)	(b)	(c)	(d)	12.	(a)	(b)	(c)	(d)	19.	(a)	(b)	(c)	(d)
6.	(a)	(b)	(c)	(d)	13.	(a)	(b)	(c)	(d)	20.	(a)	(b)	(c)	(d)
7.	(a)	(b)	(c)	(d)	14.	(a)	(b)	(c)	(d)					

▶ Section 2

1.	(a)	(b)	(c)	(d)	8.	(a)	(b)	(c)	(d)	15.	(a)	(b)	(c)	(d)
2.	(a)	(b)	(c)	(d)	9.	(a)	(b)	(c)	(d)	16.	(a)	(b)	(c)	(d)
3.	(a)	(b)	(c)	(d)	10.	(a)	(b)	(c)	(d)	17.	(a)	(b)	(c)	(d)
4.	(a)	(b)	(c)	(d)	11.	(a)	(b)	(c)	(d)	18.	(a)	(b)	(c)	(d)
5.	(a)	(b)	(c)	(d)	12.	(a)	(b)	(c)	(d)	19.	(a)	(b)	(c)	(d)
6.	(a)	(b)	(c)	(d)	13.	(a)	(b)	(c)	(d)	20.	(a)	(b)	(c)	(d)
7.	(a)	(b)	(c)	(d)	14.	(a)	(b)	(c)	(d)					

▶ Section 3

1.	(a)(b)(c)(d)(e)(f)(g)(h)	8.	(a)(b)(c)(d)(e)(f)(g)(h)	15.	(a)(b)(c)(d)(e)(f)
2.	(a)(b)(c)(d)(e)(f)(g)(h)	9.	(a)(b)(c)(d)(e)	16.	(a)(b)(c)(d)(e)(f)
3.	(a)(b)(c)(d)(e)(f)(g)	10.	(a)(b)(c)(d)(e)(f)	17.	(a)(b)(c)(d)(e)(f)(g)
4.	(a)(b)(c)(d)(e)(f)	11.	(a)(b)(c)(d)(e)(f)(g)	18.	(a)(b)(c)(d)(e)
5.	(a)(b)(c)(d)(e)(f)(g)	12.	(a)(b)(c)(d)(e)	19.	(a)(b)(c)(d)(e)(f)
6.	(a)(b)(c)(d)(e)	13.	(a)(b)(c)(d)(e)(f)(g)	20.	(a)(b)(c)(d)(e)
7.	(a)(b)(c)(d)(e)(f)	14.	(a)(b)(c)(d)(e)(f)(g)		

▶ Personal Characteristics and Experience Inventory

Section One

Following is a list of statements people might make about themselves. Read each statement and decide if it applies to you. You have four options: "Strongly Agree," "Agree," "Disagree," and "Strongly Disagree."

1. I would like to manage the work of a department or team.
   a. Strongly Agree
   b. Agree
   c. Disagree
   d. Strongly Disagree

2. I would like to help people learn to cope with their problems.
   a. Strongly Agree
   b. Agree
   c. Disagree
   d. Strongly Disagree

3. The work of a research scientist must be very boring.
   a. Strongly Agree
   b. Agree
   c. Disagree
   d. Strongly Disagree

4. It is all right to take pencils, paper clips, or other small items home from work for one's own use.
   a. Strongly Agree
   b. Agree
   c. Disagree
   d. Strongly Disagree

5. I would not like the work of a school teacher.
   a. Strongly Agree
   b. Agree
   c. Disagree
   d. Strongly Disagree

6. I enjoy trying to fix broken appliances.
   a. Strongly Agree
   b. Agree
   c. Disagree
   d. Strongly Disagree

7. I would like a clearly defined job where I know exactly what needs to be done.
   a. Strongly Agree
   b. Agree
   c. Disagree
   d. Strongly Disagree

8. I would enjoy working for a musical group or at a theater where concerts are performed.
   a. Strongly Agree
   b. Agree
   c. Disagree
   d. Strongly Disagree

9. I get stressed when keeping track of lots of details.
   a. Strongly Agree
   b. Agree
   c. Disagree
   d. Strongly Disagree

10. Selling products for a commission would be a scary way to earn a living.
    a. Strongly Agree
    b. Agree
    c. Disagree
    d. Strongly Disagree

11. Operating power machinery is a pain in the neck.
   a. Strongly Agree
   b. Agree
   c. Disagree
   d. Strongly Disagree

12. I enjoy getting people to do what I want.
   a. Strongly Agree
   b. Agree
   c. Disagree
   d. Strongly Disagree

13. Drawing or painting pictures has never really interested me.
   a. Strongly Agree
   b. Agree
   c. Disagree
   d. Strongly Disagree

14. I like to observe nature and try to understand natural phenomena.
   a. Strongly Agree
   b. Agree
   c. Disagree
   d. Strongly Disagree

15. I like getting a new tool and learning how to use it.
   a. Strongly Agree
   b. Agree
   c. Disagree
   d. Strongly Disagree

16. "Borrowing" money from the cash drawer or petty cash box at work can be acceptable.
   a. Strongly Agree
   b. Agree
   c. Disagree
   d. Strongly Disagree

17. I find comfort in following routines.
   a. Strongly Agree
   b. Agree
   c. Disagree
   d. Strongly Disagree

18. Healing sick people would be very rewarding.
   a. Strongly Agree
   b. Agree
   c. Disagree
   d. Strongly Disagree

19. I would find it interesting to help create advertisements or publicity brochures.
   a. Strongly Agree
   b. Agree
   c. Disagree
   d. Strongly Disagree

20. I enjoy figuring out how things work.
   a. Strongly Agree
   b. Agree
   c. Disagree
   d. Strongly Disagree

Section Two

Following is a list of things people might do and experiences people might have. Read each one and decide how often you engage in that activity or have that experience. You have four choices: "Very Often," "Often," "Sometimes," and "Rarely or Never."

1. I contribute a lot during meetings and discussions.
   a. Very Often
   b. Often
   c. Sometimes
   d. Rarely or Never

2. People can be counted on to do the job they've promised to do.
   a. Very Often
   b. Often
   c. Sometimes
   d. Rarely or Never

3. I prefer to do a job the traditional way rather than trying unusual or new methods.
   a. Very Often
   b. Often
   c. Sometimes
   d. Rarely or Never

4. I use to-do lists, day timers, and weekly planners to organize my work.
   a. Very Often
   b. Often
   c. Sometimes
   d. Rarely or Never

5. Feeling sad, blue, or "down in the dumps" interferes with my work.
   a. Very Often
   b. Often
   c. Sometimes
   d. Rarely or Never

6. Evil spirits have tried to prevent me from getting promoted at work.
   a. Very Often
   b. Often
   c. Sometimes
   d. Rarely or Never

7. I tend to work alone, without checking in with others.
   a. Very Often
   b. Often
   c. Sometimes
   d. Rarely or Never

8. People agree that I am a natural leader; they pay attention to me.
   a. Very Often
   b. Often
   c. Sometimes
   d. Rarely or Never

9. I let things go until the last minute and then work really fast to get them done.
   a. Very Often
   b. Often
   c. Sometimes
   d. Rarely or Never

10. I disagree with the ways other people want to get the job done.
   a. Very Often
   b. Often
   c. Sometimes
   d. Rarely or Never

11. I feel like I can't cope with some of my job's demands.
   a. Very Often
   b. Often
   c. Sometimes
   d. Rarely or Never

12. I clean and polish my shoes and brush the lint off my clothes before going to work.
   a. Very Often
   b. Often
   c. Sometimes
   d. Rarely or Never

13. I do what needs to be done before I do what I want to do.
   a. Very Often
   b. Often
   c. Sometimes
   d. Rarely or Never

14. People agree that I am calm under pressure.
   a. Very Often
   b. Often
   c. Sometimes
   d. Rarely or Never

15. I try to give my work a certain artistic flair, even if it takes time and effort to do so.
   a. Very Often
   b. Often
   c. Sometimes
   d. Rarely or Never

16. People I've worked with have seemed to be plotting murders or acts of terror.
   a. Very Often
   b. Often
   c. Sometimes
   d. Rarely or Never

17. I feel tempted to take shortcuts to get a task done faster, even if it means doing a sloppy job.
   a. Very Often
   b. Often
   c. Sometimes
   d. Rarely or Never

18. When someone is stuck with a problem, I'm willing to help him or her out.
   a. Very Often
   b. Often
   c. Sometimes
   d. Rarely or Never

19. People agree that I am good at finding new and different ways of getting things done.
   a. Very Often
   b. Often
   c. Sometimes
   d. Rarely or Never

20. I would feel irritated with supervisors who criticized my work.
   a. Very Often
   b. Often
   c. Sometimes
   d. Rarely or Never

Section Three

Following are a number of experiences one might have at work. Read each statement and decide which is true for you.

1. What kind of supervisor do you like most?
   a. one who is "hands off" and lets me work on my own
   b. one who is "hands off" and lets me work on my own, but is there if I need help
   c. one who tells me what needs to be done, but not when and how to do it
   d. one who tells me what needs to be done, and then checks back frequently to determine my progress
   e. one who tells me what to do and how and when to do it, but doesn't check on my progress
   f. one who tells me what to do and how and when to do it, and checks frequently on my progress
   g. would not mind any of these
   h. not sure

2. What level of decision making do you least like in your job?

   a. tasks where I frequently make tough decisions on my own

   b. tasks where I frequently make fairly straight-forward decisions on my own

   c. tasks where I occasionally make decisions on my own

   d. tasks where I frequently make decisions in consultation with others

   e. tasks where I follow the decisions of others

   f. tasks that require no decision making by anyone because they are very routine

   g. would not mind any of these

   h. not sure

3. What sort of planning strategies do you prefer to use in your work?

   a. I like planning far in advance so there are no surprises.

   b. I think both simple and complicated tasks should be planned ahead to play it safe.

   c. I only like to plan out complicated tasks.

   d. I don't like to waste my time planning ahead, as things usually change.

   e. I believe planning makes things more complicated. Why make things harder than they have to be?

   f. I have no strong feelings about how to plan things at work.

   g. not sure

4. Which type of job do you like least?

   a. a job that expects you to follow orders without questioning them

   b. a job that expects you to follow orders, but asks you for some input into the decision making

   c. a job that expects you to make decisions for yourself after consulting with others

   d. a job that expects you to make decisions for yourself without consulting with others

   e. would not mind any of these

   f. not sure

5. Which describes the work situation in which you are most comfortable?

   a. knowing that I will spend all day in the same place doing the same thing

   b. knowing that I will spend all day in the same place doing a couple of different tasks

   c. knowing that I will spend all day in the same place, doing different tasks on different days

   d. knowing that I will spend all day in the same place, doing different tasks with different people each day

   e. knowing that I will spend the day doing different tasks in different places with different people or on my own each day

   f. would not mind any of these

   g. not sure

6. In which jobs have you been happiest?

   a. jobs that require a lot of movement and activity

   b. jobs that require a moderate amount of activity

   c. jobs that allow you to stay in one place most the day with little running around

   d. would not mind any of these

   e. not sure

7. What do you feel are the worst kinds of work?

   a. where you have to figure out how to do things on your own

   b. where you have to do things you have never done before

   c. where you have to do new things but have instructions and rules to go by

   d. where you do the same thing all the time and don't need to deal with new things

   e. would not mind any of these

   f. not sure

8. In your experience, which tasks are least interesting?

   a. tasks where you have no set amount of stuff to do within a given time period and you have to keep yourself motivated to finish

   b. tasks where you have to accomplish a certain amount, but no timeline is specified

   c. tasks where you have to accomplish a certain amount within a specified amount of time

   d. tasks where you have a lot to accomplish within a short period of time

   e. tasks where you have a lot to accomplish within a short period of time and there are hardly any breaks

   f. tasks where you have a lot to accomplish within a short period of time, there are hardly any breaks, and you will get into trouble if you don't get it all done in time

   g. would not mind any of these

   h. not sure

9. Which strategy do you like to use when reading a document for work?

   a. I like to read over the document quickly to get the gist of what it is saying.

   b. I like to make note of every point made in the document as I read on.

   c. I like to read over the whole document and then go back and make note of every point.

   d. can take any of the approaches

   e. not sure

10. Which describes your preferred working environment?

   a. indoors without windows

   b. indoors with windows

   c. driving a vehicle with a little walking

   d. walking outdoors a lot, with little regard for the weather

   e. would not mind any of these

   f. not sure

11. What level of responsibility do you typically desire in your work?

   a. I prefer to manage a team of subordinates.

   b. I prefer to be a group leader among my colleagues at my level.

   c. I prefer to take charge of a project all on my own.

   d. I prefer having a boss to take the blame in case things go wrong.

   e. I don't want to be in charge of anything, just tell me what to do and I'll do it.

   f. would not mind any of these

   g. not sure

12. How do you like to approach a problem on the job?

   a. I ask someone else how to handle the situation.

   b. I look into how others have handled similar situations and then use these as a guide to develop my own solution.

   c. I try to come up with new ways to approach a problem in the hopes of coming up with better solutions.

   d. would not mind any of these strategies

   e. not sure

13. What contact with your fellow employees do you like at work?

   a. I try to organize social events for after work.

   b. I am friendly with other people at work, but don't see them after work.

   c. I feel shy at work and don't go out of my way to talk with others.

   d. I like to keep to myself.

   e. I like jobs where I am on my own and nobody can try to get into my personal business.

   f. would not mind any of these

   g. not sure

14. Which best describes how you prefer to work with others?
  a. I like working in a group, sharing ideas, responsibility, and credit for what gets done.
  b. I like working in a group because then I have others to help me out.
  c. I prefer working in groups because then I can do less work.
  d. Working in groups is difficult because each member has a different idea of how to get things done.
  e. I don't like working in groups because you can't count on others to do their fair share.
  f. It doesn't matter if I work in a group or not.
  g. not sure

15. When working on a problem, how do you think it through?
  a. The solution just pops into my head.
  b. I have to think about it for a little while, but then the solution just comes to me.
  c. I typically think things out to come up with a solution.
  d. The only way to come up with a solution is to reason things through to a logical conclusion.
  e. I would not mind using any of these strategies.
  f. not sure

16. Which kind of tasks do you prefer?
  a. I like dealing with tasks in which the correct way to accomplish it is not obvious.
  b. I like dealing with tasks that require multiple steps to completion.
  c. I like dealing with tasks in which everything is laid out and routine.
  d. I like dealing with tasks that don't require a lot of steps and are simple.
  e. I would not mind dealing with any of these tasks.
  f. not sure

17. What kind of work would you like best?
  a. data entry, typing in the same kind of information for each piece of paper
  b. moving boxes from one location to another
  c. driving or walking on the same route every day
  d. handling different service needs for customers at one location
  e. would not mind any of these
  f. would not like any of these
  g. not sure

18. How do you typically respond to the pressure of deadlines?
  a. If I don't have a deadline, I won't get the job done.
  b. I like to give myself deadlines, if they don't already exist, because it motivates me to do the work.
  c. Deadlines overwhelm me and make an easy task unmanageable.
  d. Deadlines don't influence my ability to get the work done.
  e. not sure

19. Which of the following describes your preferred level of customer service?
  a. I want to work with customers all day handling a variety of needs.
  b. I would prefer to spend only part of my day on customer service.
  c. I like working on my own or with colleagues with minimal customer service.
  d. I prefer not to have to work with customers at all.
  e. would not mind any of these
  f. not sure

20. Which is an ideal work schedule?
  a. working during the day only
  b. working at night only
  c. rotating day and night shifts
  d. would not mind any of these
  e. not sure

▶ Scoring Instructions

Section One

This section measures six types of occupational interest. It also includes two questions that ask about honesty on the job. Write the score shown for each of your answers in the space to the right of the item. Then, add the scores for each interest or characteristic. The higher the score, the more the characteristic describes you. It is very likely that you will obtain high scores on two or even three interests. This is normal. It means that they have some of the characteristics of each of the interest types you endorsed.

Please note that this is only an example of these types of measures. There are too few of these example questions to be a reliable and valid measure.

Realistic: 6, 11, and 15

People with Realistic interests are practical people who like to solve practical problems. They tend to enjoy working with tools, machines, and motor vehicles and like learning how to operate mechanical devices. They tend to be physically active and value strength and agility. Some also like working with animals, especially large animals like cattle. Many postal service jobs involve working with machines or motor vehicles.

#6: $a = 3, b = 2, c = 1, d = 0$	_____
#11: $a = 0, b = 1, c = 2, d = 3$	_____
#15: $a = 3, b = 2, c = 1, d = 0$	_____
Total Score:	_____

Investigative: 3, 14, and 20

People with Investigative interests enjoy learning for its own sake. They are especially likely to enjoy mathematics or science. They like to read about these subjects and try solving scientific problems. They tend to want to develop their logical faculties rather than physical skills. In many cases, they prefer to work independently, with minimal supervision and loose deadlines.

#3: $a = 3, b = 2, c = 1, d = 0$	_____
#14: $a = 3, b = 2, c = 1, d = 0$	_____
#20: $a = 3, b = 2, c = 1, d = 0$	_____
Total Score:	_____

Artistic: 8, 13, and 19

People with Artistic interests want to express themselves freely, typically through art, music, or writing. In order to do so more effectively, they want to cultivate their skills with the instruments used in their chosen media, such as oil paints, pianos, or language arts. They set a high value on originality. They do not like being expected to follow a routine, a strict schedule, or a set of company rules.

#8: $a = 3, b = 2, c = 1, d = 0$	_____
#13: $a = 0, b = 1, c = 2, d = 3$	_____
#19: $a = 3, b = 2, c = 1, d = 0$	_____
Total Score:	_____

Social: 2, 5, and 18

People with Social interests enjoy working with people, especially as part of a team or discussion group—not so much as part of an authority hierarchy. They usually want their work to be helpful to others in some way. Many choose careers in education, healthcare, child care, or social work. They tend to be verbally skilled but not mechanically inclined. Customer service jobs involve a social element.

#2: $a = 3, b = 2, c = 1, d = 0$	_____
#5: $a = 0, b = 1, c = 2, d = 3$	_____
#18: $a = 3, b = 2, c = 1, d = 0$	_____
Total Score:	_____

Enterprising: 1, 10, and 12

People with Enterprising interests enjoy working with other people with the objective of persuading them to do things that will advance personal or organizational goals. They like to manage. They like to sell. They like to acquire power, status, and wealth. Many choose careers in sales or management, especially in areas where lots of money can be made. They can have a hard time with entry-level or "dead end" positions.

#1:	a = 3, b = 2, c = 1, d = 0	_____
#10:	a = 0, b = 1, c = 2, d = 3	_____
#12:	a = 3, b = 2, c = 1, d = 0	_____
Total Score:		_____

Conventional: 7, 9, and 17

People with Conventional interests prefer clear rules and a working environment where they feel in control. They value being dependable and organized. They tend to be good with clerical and numerical tasks, and to be interested in money. Leading orderly work lives, keeping accurate records, and following directions or standard guidelines all are important to these people. They tend to do well operating office equipment, too. Many postal service jobs are well suited to people with Conventional interests.

#7:	a = 3, b = 2, c = 1, d = 0	_____
#9:	a = 0, b = 1, c = 2, d = 3	_____
#17:	a = 3, b = 2, c = 1, d = 0	_____
Total Score:		_____

Dishonesty Items: 4 and 16

If you agreed with either of these statements, your candidacy is likely to be highly questioned. Note that even admitting to very mild violations of honesty—such as bringing home a pencil—could count strongly against you.

#4:	a = 3, b = 2, c = 1, d = 0	_____
#16:	a = 3, b = 2, c = 1, d = 0	_____
Total Score:		_____

Section Two

This section measures five major personality traits. It also includes three items that measure how much you are distorting your answers in the hope of presenting yourself more favorably, and two items that measure strange or bizarre ideas. Write the score shown for each of your answers in the space to the right of the item. Then, add the scores for each trait or characteristic. The higher the score, the more the trait is characteristic of you. The five major traits are all normal. Everybody has each one to some degree. They are also unrelated to each other. You can obtain very high (or low) scores on any combination of these traits. Please note that this is only an example of these types of measures. There are too few of these example questions to be a reliable and valid measure.

Extraversion: 1, 7, and 8

People high in Extraversion are sociable, active, assertive, and cheerful. People low in Extraversion are more private, reserved, and sober-minded. It is not "better" to be one or the other. Each has its advantages. But different jobs may be better suited to people high or low in Extraversion.

#1:	a = 3, b = 2, c = 1, d = 0	
#7:	a = 0, b = 1, c = 2, d = 3	
#8:	a = 3, b = 2, c = 1, d = 0	
Total Score:		

Emotional Stability: 5, 11, and 14

People high in Stability are secure, calm, and handle stress well. People low in Stability are inclined to worry, suffer from anxiety, depression, or irritability, and generally feel insecure about themselves. Very low levels of Stability can be a problem, especially in high-stress situations. But low levels of Stability do not mean that a person is mentally ill—just about everybody experiences some signs of instability.

#5: a = 0, b = 1, c = 2, d = 3 _____
#11: a = 0, b = 1, c = 2, d = 3 _____
#14: a = 3, b = 2, c = 1, d = 0 _____
Total Score: _____

Agreeableness: 2, 10, and 18

People high in Agreeableness tend to be helpful, cooperative, trusting, and likable. People low in Agreeableness tend to be more cynical and "crotchety." On the other hand, people low in this trait also may be more independent and better able to say no to unreasonable requests. Once again, then, normal people may be high or low in this trait, and neither is inherently superior—although level of Agreeableness may be a factor in job *placement*.

#2: a = 3, b = 2, c = 1, d = 0 _____
#10: a = 0, b = 1, c = 2, d = 3 _____
#18: a = 3, b = 2, c = 1, d = 0 _____
Total Score: _____

Conscientiousness: 4, 9, and 13

People high in Conscientiousness are careful, organized, and self-disciplined. They are likely to be careful to "get the job done, and done right," though sometimes they may be too focused on getting every detail perfect. People low in Conscientiousness are more relaxed about life and probably have more fun, but also tend to be disorganized and less reliable. Very low levels of Conscientiousness are likely to be a problem in many jobs, even though there is nothing abnormal about having low levels of this trait.

#4: a = 3, b = 2, c = 1, d = 0 _____
#9: a = 0, b = 1, c = 2, d = 3 _____
#13: a = 3, b = 2, c = 1, d = 0 _____
Total Score: _____

Openness to Experience: 3, 15, and 19

People high in Openness to Experience tend to be imaginative people who crave and enjoy lots of variety in their lives. Many are interested in the arts. They tend to be open to views and lifestyles different from their own and to be impatient with routines. People low in Openness to Experience are more traditional or practical and tend to have narrower interests and views on life. Once again, it is normal to be either high or low on this trait.

#3: a = 0, b = 1, c = 2, d = 3 _____
#15: a = 3, b = 2, c = 1, d = 0 _____
#19: a = 3, b = 2, c = 1, d = 0 _____
Total Score: _____

Social Desirability: 12, 17, and 20

People high in Social Desirability very much want to be viewed favorably by others. As a result, they tend to present themselves in a positive light—sometimes unrealistically so. If a person scores very high on Social Desirability, a personnel officer might think that their scores on other traits are distorted. On the other hand, most people looking for work will say some nice things about themselves. Do not try to "spot" social desirability items. Just answer honestly and you will not be caught in any lies.

#12: a = 3, b = 2, c = 1, d = 0 _____
#17: a = 0, b = 1, c = 2, d = 3 _____
#20: a = 0, b = 1, c = 2, d = 3 _____
Total Score: _____

Bizarre Ideation: 6 and 16

These items relate to very unusual—even bizarre—ways of thinking or acting. Few people believe that evil spirits are trying to thwart their careers, for example.

#6: a = 3, b = 2, c = 1, d = 0 _____
#16: a = 3, b = 2, c = 1, d = 0 _____
Total Score: _____

SUMMARY OF PERSONAL CHARACTERISTICS SCORES		
OCCUPATIONAL INTERESTS	**PERSONALITY TRAITS**	**OTHER MEASURES**
Realistic: _____	Extraversion: _____	Social Desirability: _____
Investigative: _____	Emotional Stability: _____	Dishonesty: _____
Artistic: _____	Agreeableness: _____	Bizarre Ideation: _____
Social: _____	Conscientiousness: _____	
Enterprising: _____	Openness: _____	
Conventional: _____		

What Do My Personal Characteristics Scores Mean?

You should not read too much into your scores on this practice test. Here is why: The scores you added up are what are known as *raw scores*. Your raw score has no meaning in and of itself. It has meaning only when compared to the scores obtained by a large number of other people. These provide *norms* for a test; norms are the standards against which a person's scores are compared. The easiest kind of norm to understand is a *percentile score*. What percent of people obtain scores higher than yours? Without a set of norms, you cannot tell, for example, whether a score of 6 on Realistic interests is high, average, or low. (Even if you knew that, you would not know what the Postal Service is looking for!) Once again, we must stress this point: Do not assume you know enough about a personal characteristics test to be able to obtain the scores most likely to get you hired. The rule remains: Be honest and straightforward.

Section Three

This section measures which type of work experiences you would be most comfortable with in your job. There are 20 different constructs that are combined to determine a profile for your preferred work experience. This information can then be used to determine which of the entry-level positions at the post office might suit you best. Determine whether your answer fits the profile for each of the constructs and check "yes" or "no" in the space to the right of the item. Then, add the number of "yes" responses for each job position profile. If you answered "yes" to the majority of questions in a profile, you would probably be a good match for that position. It is possible that you will be well suited to more than one position or to none of these entry-level positions.

<u>City Carrier:</u> Deliver and collect mail on foot or by vehicle providing customer service in an assigned territory.

ITEM CONSTRUCT	ANSWER FITTING PROFILE	MY ANSWER FITS PROFILE	
#1 Management	a	_____ yes	_____ no
#2 Decision Making	a, d, e, f	_____ yes	_____ no
#3 Planning	a, b	_____ yes	_____ no
#4 Autonomy	a, b, c	_____ yes	_____ no
#6 Activity	a, b	_____ yes	_____ no
#9 Detail Oriented	b, c	_____ yes	_____ no
#10 Outdoors	e, f	_____ yes	_____ no
#11 Responsibility	a, b, c	_____ yes	_____ no
#14 Team Work	d, e	_____ yes	_____ no
#17 Repetitive Tasks	c, e	_____ yes	_____ no
#19 Customer Service	a, b, c	_____ yes	_____ no
#20 Shift Work	a	_____ yes	_____ no
	Total Number of Yes Responses:	_____	

<u>Mail Handler:</u> Load and unload containers of mail, open and empty containers of mail in various locations in the building.

ITEM CONSTRUCT	ANSWER FITTING PROFILE	MY ANSWER FITS PROFILE	
#1 Management	d, e, f	_____ yes	_____ no
#2 Decision Making	a, b, c, d	_____ yes	_____ no
#4 Autonomy	c, d	_____ yes	_____ no
#5 Task Variety	a, b	_____ yes	_____ no
#6 Activity	a	_____ yes	_____ no
#7 Challenging	a, b	_____ yes	_____ no
#8 Fast Pace	a, b, c	_____ yes	_____ no
#10 Outdoors	a	_____ yes	_____ no
#11 Responsibility	d, e	_____ yes	_____ no

#12 Creative Thinking	a	yes	no
#16 Simple Tasks	c, d	yes	no
#17 Repetitive Tasks	b, e	yes	no
#18 Deadlines	a, b	yes	no
#19 Customer Service	d	yes	no
#20 Shift Work	c, d	yes	no

Total Number of Yes Responses:

<u>Mail Processing Clerk:</u> Operate and monitor automated mail processing equipment or anually sort mail. Must collate, bundle, and transfer mail to appropriate locations.

ITEM CONSTRUCT	ANSWER FITTING PROFILE	MY ANSWER FITS PROFILE	
#1 Management	d, e, f	yes	no
#2 Decision Making	a, b, c, d	yes	no
#4 Autonomy	c, d	yes	no
#5 Task Variety	a, b	yes	no
#6 Activity	c	yes	no
#7 Challenging	a, b	yes	no
#8 Fast Pace	a, b, c	yes	no
#9 Detail Oriented	b, c	yes	no
#10 Outdoors	a	yes	no
#11 Responsibility	d, e	yes	no
#12 Creative Thinking	a	yes	no
#16 Simple Tasks	c, d	yes	no
#17 Repetitive Tasks	a, e	yes	no
#18 Deadlines	a, b	yes	no
#19 Customer Service	d	yes	no
#20 Shift Work	c, d	yes	no

Total Number of Yes Responses:

<u>Sales, Service, and Distribution Associate:</u> Interact with customers selling products and providing support, as well as distributing mail.

ITEM CONSTRUCT	ANSWER FITTING PROFILE	MY ANSWER FITS PROFILE	
#1 Management	a, b, c	_____ yes	_____ no
#2 Decision Making	a, d, e, f	_____ yes	_____ no
#3 Planning	a, b	_____ yes	_____ no
#4 Autonomy	a, b, c	_____ yes	_____ no
#5 Task Variety	c, d, e	_____ yes	_____ no
#9 Detail Oriented	b, c	_____ yes	_____ no
#10 Outdoors	a, b	_____ yes	_____ no
#11 Responsibility	a, b, c	_____ yes	_____ no
#13 Social Interaction	a, b	_____ yes	_____ no
#17 Repetitive Tasks	d, e	_____ yes	_____ no
#19 Customer Service	a	_____ yes	_____ no
#20 Shift Work	a	_____ yes	_____ no
	Total Number of Yes Responses:	_____	

The following profile suggests that you may not be a good match for any of the entry-level positions at the post office.

ITEM CONSTRUCT	ANSWER FITTING PROFILE	MY ANSWER FITS PROFILE	
#2 Decision Making	e, f	_____ yes	_____ no
#4 Autonomy	a	_____ yes	_____ no
#7 Challenging	d	_____ yes	_____ no
#9 Detail Oriented	a	_____ yes	_____ no
#12 Creative Thinking	c	_____ yes	_____ no
#14 Team Work	a	_____ yes	_____ no
#15 Intuitive Cognitive Style	a	_____ yes	_____ no
#16 Complicated Tasks	a	_____ yes	_____ no
#17 Repetitive Tasks	f	_____ yes	_____ no
#18 Deadlines	c	_____ yes	_____ no
	Total Number of Yes Responses:	_____	

What Do My Experiences Scores Mean?

Again, we must caution you that this questionnaire is only an example of the kinds of questions the USPS might include in its inventory. It is not known exactly what the USPS has included in its measure or how it uses the information. The previous questions are meant to give you a feel for the test, but do not necessarily measure the same constructs or compile the position profiles in the same manner.

▶ Benefits of Using Psychological Testing for Selection and Placement

Using inventories such as the USPS Test 473 Part D—Personal Characteristics and Experience Inventory—provides a number of advantages for the employer. This type of test is more objective than other traditional assessments used in the hiring process, such as interviews and letters of recommendation. Additionally, using paper-and-pencil tests is more efficient in that it allows many people to be tested at the same time using fewer resources, and allows for comparison of scores across candidates.

Research examining the relationship between personality and work behavior of employed persons suggests that for the "big five" personality traits: Conscientiousness predicts high performance across many types of jobs; Extraversion predicts high performance for managerial and sales positions; Openness predicts taking well to training; and people who are employed fall within a restricted range on Agreeableness and Emotional Stability, perhaps because those who score on the low end on these traits are typically not employed.

Tests that focus on one's interests are used with the assumption that matching one's interests to one's position will lead to better performance, increased productivity, and greater satisfaction. Interests are related to six personality occupational types: Realistic, Investigative, Artistic, Social, Enterprising, and Conventional (RIASEC). There is some overlap between the "big five" personality traits and RIASEC, but they are distinct and uniquely contribute to the prediction of job success.

Practice Postal
Worker Exam 2

CHAPTER SUMMARY

This is the second of four practice exams in this book based on Test 473, the Postal Worker Exam. After working through the instructional material in the previous chapters, take this test to see how much your score has improved since you took the first exam.

Like the practice exam in Chapter 4, the exam that follows is based on Test 473, the exam given to applicants for many entry-level jobs with the USPS. Remember that because Part D contains only questions that are based on your opinion and experience, it is not included in this practice test. To learn about these questions and to evaluate your responses, review Chapter 8.

Before you start this test, you should have read the review materials found in Chapters 5–7. You should also simulate the actual test-taking experience as closely as possible. You should have a stopwatch or clock available to time yourself on each part of the exam.

The only other things you need before you begin the test are a quiet place to work, No. 2 pencils, and enough time to complete the test at one sitting—about an hour, including a few minutes for a break between each part.

The answer sheet you should use for answering the questions is on pages 117–118. Then comes the exam itself, and after that is the answer key. The answer key is followed by a section on how to score your exam.

▶ Part A: Address Checking

1.	ⓐ	ⓑ	ⓒ	ⓓ		21.	ⓐ	ⓑ	ⓒ	ⓓ		41.	ⓐ	ⓑ	ⓒ	ⓓ
2.	ⓐ	ⓑ	ⓒ	ⓓ		22.	ⓐ	ⓑ	ⓒ	ⓓ		42.	ⓐ	ⓑ	ⓒ	ⓓ
3.	ⓐ	ⓑ	ⓒ	ⓓ		23.	ⓐ	ⓑ	ⓒ	ⓓ		43.	ⓐ	ⓑ	ⓒ	ⓓ
4.	ⓐ	ⓑ	ⓒ	ⓓ		24.	ⓐ	ⓑ	ⓒ	ⓓ		44.	ⓐ	ⓑ	ⓒ	ⓓ
5.	ⓐ	ⓑ	ⓒ	ⓓ		25.	ⓐ	ⓑ	ⓒ	ⓓ		45.	ⓐ	ⓑ	ⓒ	ⓓ
6.	ⓐ	ⓑ	ⓒ	ⓓ		26.	ⓐ	ⓑ	ⓒ	ⓓ		46.	ⓐ	ⓑ	ⓒ	ⓓ
7.	ⓐ	ⓑ	ⓒ	ⓓ		27.	ⓐ	ⓑ	ⓒ	ⓓ		47.	ⓐ	ⓑ	ⓒ	ⓓ
8.	ⓐ	ⓑ	ⓒ	ⓓ		28.	ⓐ	ⓑ	ⓒ	ⓓ		48.	ⓐ	ⓑ	ⓒ	ⓓ
9.	ⓐ	ⓑ	ⓒ	ⓓ		29.	ⓐ	ⓑ	ⓒ	ⓓ		49.	ⓐ	ⓑ	ⓒ	ⓓ
10.	ⓐ	ⓑ	ⓒ	ⓓ		30.	ⓐ	ⓑ	ⓒ	ⓓ		50.	ⓐ	ⓑ	ⓒ	ⓓ
11.	ⓐ	ⓑ	ⓒ	ⓓ		31.	ⓐ	ⓑ	ⓒ	ⓓ		51.	ⓐ	ⓑ	ⓒ	ⓓ
12.	ⓐ	ⓑ	ⓒ	ⓓ		32.	ⓐ	ⓑ	ⓒ	ⓓ		52.	ⓐ	ⓑ	ⓒ	ⓓ
13.	ⓐ	ⓑ	ⓒ	ⓓ		33.	ⓐ	ⓑ	ⓒ	ⓓ		53.	ⓐ	ⓑ	ⓒ	ⓓ
14.	ⓐ	ⓑ	ⓒ	ⓓ		34.	ⓐ	ⓑ	ⓒ	ⓓ		54.	ⓐ	ⓑ	ⓒ	ⓓ
15.	ⓐ	ⓑ	ⓒ	ⓓ		35.	ⓐ	ⓑ	ⓒ	ⓓ		55.	ⓐ	ⓑ	ⓒ	ⓓ
16.	ⓐ	ⓑ	ⓒ	ⓓ		36.	ⓐ	ⓑ	ⓒ	ⓓ		56.	ⓐ	ⓑ	ⓒ	ⓓ
17.	ⓐ	ⓑ	ⓒ	ⓓ		37.	ⓐ	ⓑ	ⓒ	ⓓ		57.	ⓐ	ⓑ	ⓒ	ⓓ
18.	ⓐ	ⓑ	ⓒ	ⓓ		38.	ⓐ	ⓑ	ⓒ	ⓓ		58.	ⓐ	ⓑ	ⓒ	ⓓ
19.	ⓐ	ⓑ	ⓒ	ⓓ		39.	ⓐ	ⓑ	ⓒ	ⓓ		59.	ⓐ	ⓑ	ⓒ	ⓓ
20.	ⓐ	ⓑ	ⓒ	ⓓ		40.	ⓐ	ⓑ	ⓒ	ⓓ		60.	ⓐ	ⓑ	ⓒ	ⓓ

▶ Part B: Forms Completion

1.	ⓐ	ⓑ	ⓒ	ⓓ		11.	ⓐ	ⓑ	ⓒ	ⓓ		21.	ⓐ	ⓑ	ⓒ	ⓓ
2.	ⓐ	ⓑ	ⓒ	ⓓ		12.	ⓐ	ⓑ	ⓒ	ⓓ		22.	ⓐ	ⓑ	ⓒ	ⓓ
3.	ⓐ	ⓑ	ⓒ	ⓓ		13.	ⓐ	ⓑ	ⓒ	ⓓ		23.	ⓐ	ⓑ	ⓒ	ⓓ
4.	ⓐ	ⓑ	ⓒ	ⓓ		14.	ⓐ	ⓑ	ⓒ	ⓓ		24.	ⓐ	ⓑ	ⓒ	ⓓ
5.	ⓐ	ⓑ	ⓒ	ⓓ		15.	ⓐ	ⓑ	ⓒ	ⓓ		25.	ⓐ	ⓑ	ⓒ	ⓓ
6.	ⓐ	ⓑ	ⓒ	ⓓ		16.	ⓐ	ⓑ	ⓒ	ⓓ		26.	ⓐ	ⓑ	ⓒ	ⓓ
7.	ⓐ	ⓑ	ⓒ	ⓓ		17.	ⓐ	ⓑ	ⓒ	ⓓ		27.	ⓐ	ⓑ	ⓒ	ⓓ
8.	ⓐ	ⓑ	ⓒ	ⓓ		18.	ⓐ	ⓑ	ⓒ	ⓓ		28.	ⓐ	ⓑ	ⓒ	ⓓ
9.	ⓐ	ⓑ	ⓒ	ⓓ		19.	ⓐ	ⓑ	ⓒ	ⓓ		29.	ⓐ	ⓑ	ⓒ	ⓓ
10.	ⓐ	ⓑ	ⓒ	ⓓ		20.	ⓐ	ⓑ	ⓒ	ⓓ		30.	ⓐ	ⓑ	ⓒ	ⓓ

▶ Part C: Section 1–Coding

1. (a) (b) (c) (d)
2. (a) (b) (c) (d)
3. (a) (b) (c) (d)
4. (a) (b) (c) (d)
5. (a) (b) (c) (d)
6. (a) (b) (c) (d)
7. (a) (b) (c) (d)
8. (a) (b) (c) (d)
9. (a) (b) (c) (d)
10. (a) (b) (c) (d)
11. (a) (b) (c) (d)
12. (a) (b) (c) (d)

13. (a) (b) (c) (d)
14. (a) (b) (c) (d)
15. (a) (b) (c) (d)
16. (a) (b) (c) (d)
17. (a) (b) (c) (d)
18. (a) (b) (c) (d)
19. (a) (b) (c) (d)
20. (a) (b) (c) (d)
21. (a) (b) (c) (d)
22. (a) (b) (c) (d)
23. (a) (b) (c) (d)
24. (a) (b) (c) (d)

25. (a) (b) (c) (d)
26. (a) (b) (c) (d)
27. (a) (b) (c) (d)
28. (a) (b) (c) (d)
29. (a) (b) (c) (d)
30. (a) (b) (c) (d)
31. (a) (b) (c) (d)
32. (a) (b) (c) (d)
33. (a) (b) (c) (d)
34. (a) (b) (c) (d)
35. (a) (b) (c) (d)
36. (a) (b) (c) (d)

▶ Part C: Section 2–Memory

37. (a) (b) (c) (d)
38. (a) (b) (c) (d)
39. (a) (b) (c) (d)
40. (a) (b) (c) (d)
41. (a) (b) (c) (d)
42. (a) (b) (c) (d)
43. (a) (b) (c) (d)
44. (a) (b) (c) (d)
45. (a) (b) (c) (d)
46. (a) (b) (c) (d)
47. (a) (b) (c) (d)
48. (a) (b) (c) (d)

49. (a) (b) (c) (d)
50. (a) (b) (c) (d)
51. (a) (b) (c) (d)
52. (a) (b) (c) (d)
53. (a) (b) (c) (d)
54. (a) (b) (c) (d)
55. (a) (b) (c) (d)
56. (a) (b) (c) (d)
57. (a) (b) (c) (d)
58. (a) (b) (c) (d)
59. (a) (b) (c) (d)
60. (a) (b) (c) (d)

61. (a) (b) (c) (d)
62. (a) (b) (c) (d)
63. (a) (b) (c) (d)
64. (a) (b) (c) (d)
65. (a) (b) (c) (d)
66. (a) (b) (c) (d)
67. (a) (b) (c) (d)
68. (a) (b) (c) (d)
69. (a) (b) (c) (d)
70. (a) (b) (c) (d)
71. (a) (b) (c) (d)
72. (a) (b) (c) (d)

▶ Practice Postal Worker Exam 2

Part A—Address Checking

Directions: Review and compare the information in the **List to Be Checked** with the information in the **Correct List**. To answer each question, you must decide if there are **No errors (a)**, an error in the **Address only (b)**, an error in the **ZIP code only (c)**, or an error in **Both (d)** the address and the ZIP code. This part has 60 questions.

Time: 11 minutes

	CORRECT LIST		LIST TO BE CHECKED	
QUESTION	**ADDRESS**	**ZIP CODE**	**ADDRESS**	**ZIP CODE**
1.	710 Holloway St Kadoka, SD	57543	710 Holliday St Kadoka, SD	57534
2.	2109 Gunther Ave Jessup, MD	20794	2109 Gunther Ave Jessup, MD	20774
3.	1201 Myrtle Avenue Eastanollee, GA	30538-0584	1201 Myrtle Avenue Eastanol, GA	30538-0544
4.	2449 Shady Glen Ct Declo, ID	83323	2449 Shady Glen Ct Declo, ID	83323
5.	512 N Vanderhorst Dr Annada, MO	63330	51 N Vanderhorst Dr Annada, MO	63030
6.	1845 Cross Park Wy Dearing, KS	67340-1264	1845 Cross Park Wy Dearing, KS	67340-1264
7.	8943 Walnut Boulevard Fairview, NC	28730	8443 Walnut Boulevard Fairview, NC	28730
8.	6 Airport Way Kamiah, ID	83536	26 Airport Way Kamiah, ID	83536
9.	231 Park Place Leon, WV	25123-2573	231 Park Place Leon, WV	25123-2573
10.	1211 Wainwright Cr Mechanicsville, IA	52306-3468	1211 Wainwright Cr Mechanicsville, IA	52306-3448
11.	7883 W Foster Dr New Windsor, MD	21776	7883 W Forster Rd New Windsor, MD	27176

a. No errors
b. Address only
c. ZIP code only
d. Both

	CORRECT LIST		LIST TO BE CHECKED	
QUESTION	ADDRESS	ZIP CODE	ADDRESS	ZIP CODE
12.	5723 16th Avenue NE Poplar, WI	54864	5723 16th Avenue NE Poplar, WI	58464
13.	1016 Blythe Court W Salem, AR	72576	1016 Blythe Court N Salem, AR	72576
14.	402 Lorna Drive Snyder, NE	68664	402 Lorma Drive Snyder, NE	68664
15.	3521 Richland Ave S Susie, KY	42633	3521 Richland Ave S Susie, KY	42333
16.	8236 Melvin St Vancleave, MS	39565	8236 Melvin St Vancleave, MI	39655
17.	6348 Leicester Hwy Urbana, OH	43078	6348 Leicester Hwy Urbana, OK	43078
18.	1290 Brannon Rd Lysite, WY	82642-4356	1290 Brannon Rd Lysite, WY	82642
19.	237 Jones Mill Road Keauhou, HI	96739	237 Jones Mill Road Keauhou, HI	96139
20.	311 Camino Grande Kanosh, UT	84637	311 Camino Grande Kanosh, UT	84637
21.	5519 Ludlow Terr Kiel, WI	53042	5119 Ludlow Terr Kiel, WI	50342
22.	312 Haverford Pl Miamisburg, OH	45343-0097	213 Haverford Pl Miamisburg, OH	45343-0097
23.	2110 37th Street Lingo, NM	88123	2110 37th Street Lingo, NM	81123
24.	923 Williams Cir San Diego, CA	92037	923 Williams Cir San Diego, CA	92037
25.	PO Box 517 Longleaf, LA	71448	PO Box 157 Longleaf, LA	71448
26.	45 N Woods Rd Meacham, OR	97859	451 Woods Rd Meacham, OR	98759

a. No errors
b. Address only
c. ZIP code only
d. Both

	CORRECT LIST		LIST TO BE CHECKED	
QUESTION	**ADDRESS**	**ZIP CODE**	**ADDRESS**	**ZIP CODE**
27.	204 Cohen Hall Norway, SC	29113	204 Colen Hall Norway, SC	29113
28.	2211 Robert Rd Pittsburgh, PA	15295-3572	2211 Robert Ave Pittsburgh, PA	15295-3572
29.	2020 Beech Avenue Saint Jo, TX	76265-4521	2020 Beach Avenue Saint Jo, TX	76265-4521
30.	31 Abington Ave Sag Harbor, NY	11963	31 Abingdon Ave Sag Harbor, NY	11993
31.	6202 Ledge Mtn Road Philippi, WV	26416-3656	6202 Ledge Mtn Road Philippi, WV	26416-3655
32.	2002 Westminister Dr Oxford, ME	04270	2002 Westminister Dr Oxford, MI	04270
33.	827 Warner Boulevard Lena, WI	54139	827 Warnett Boulevard Lena, WI	45139
34.	1524 22nd Avenue Graytown, OH	43432	1524 22nd Avenue Grayson, OH	43432
35.	727 Housman St Capitan, NM	88316	727 Housman St Capitan, NM	83316
36.	2784 Fleetwood Ave Backus, MN	56435	2784 Fleetwood Ave Backus, MI	56445
37.	3356 Andrews Avenue Abac, GA	31794	3356 Andrews Avenue Abac, GA	37194
38.	363 Cornwallis Dr Chatham, NH	03813	333 Cornwallis Dr Chatham, NH	03813
39.	5418 Pheasant Dr Scranton, PA	15840	5418 Pleasant Dr Scranton, PA	18540
40.	1868 Jenny Lane Jenny Lake, WY	83012	1868 Jeanne Lane Jenny Lake, WY	83021
41.	6001 Woodland Dr Cabot, AR	72023	6001 Woodland Dr Cabot, AK	72022

a. No errors

b. Address only

c. ZIP code only

d. Both

	CORRECT LIST		LIST TO BE CHECKED	
QUESTION	ADDRESS	ZIP CODE	ADDRESS	ZIP CODE
42.	7619 Osborne Ave Adamsville, RI	02801-2462	7619 Osbourne Ave Adamsville, RI	02801-2462
43.	450 W Neck Road Finlayson, MN	55735	450 W Neck Road Finlayson, MN	55535
44.	1011 Dartmouth Place Mays Landing, NJ	08330	1011 Dartmouth Lane Mays Landing, NJ	08330
45.	2619 Val Halla Road Maumee, OH	43537	2619 Val Halla Road Maumee, OH	43537
46.	5712 Carson Pl Placedo, TX	77977-3557	5712 Carson Pl Placedo, TX	77977-3577
47.	860 Murfreesboro Pl Wildie, KY	40492	880 Murfreesboro Pl Wildie, KY	44092
48.	5858 Bonnybrier St Paulina, LA	70763	5858 Bonnybrier St Paulina, LA	70763
49.	4316 Longfellow Street Birds, IL	62415	4316 Marshmallow Street Birds, IL	64255
50.	7856 Tamerlane Ave Anvik, AK	99558-2464	7856 Tamellan Ave Anvik, AK	99558-6424
51.	3942 Wildwood Cir Charlo, MT	59824	3942 Wildwood Court Charlo, MT	59824
52.	3555 Boundary Road Harbor Point, MI	49740	3555 Boundary Road Harbor Point, MI	49740
53.	103 Hillwood Boulevard Hytop, AL	35768	103 Hillwood Boulevard Hytop, AL	37568
54.	6669 Winslow Place Meally, KY	41234	6669 Winslow Place Meally, KS	41234
55.	9784 Starboard Dr Rebuck, PA	17867	9784 Stebboard Dr Rebuck, PA	17867
56.	5533 Shore Road Varna, IL	61375-3636	5533 Shore Road Varna, IL	61375-6636

a. No errors

b. Address only

c. ZIP code only

d. Both

	CORRECT LIST		LIST TO BE CHECKED	
QUESTION	ADDRESS	ZIP CODE	ADDRESS	ZIP CODE
57.	108 Crickets Grove		108 Cricket Grove	
	Westfield, VT	05874	Westfield, VT	05874
58.	194 N Berwick Ln		194 N Berwick Ln	
	Zap, ND	58580	Zap, ND	58080
59.	6512 Bremen Dr		6512 Bremen Dr	
	Wren, OH	45899-4732	Wren, OK	45899-4372
60.	PO Box 58489		PO Box 58989	
	Pioneer, LA	71266-9058	Pioneer, LA	71266-9059

a. No errors
b. Address only
c. ZIP code only
d. Both

Part B—Forms Completion

Directions: Review each form and answer the 30 questions that follow.

Time: 15 minutes

Dispatch Note

A. Contents		B. Quantity	C. Weight	
			C1. lbs	C2. ozs
D. Value $				
E. Tariff Code		F. Origin of Goods (Country)		
G. Shipping Type				
G1. [ ] Priority G2. [ ] Standard G3. [ ] Other				
H. Insurance Fee				
I. License Number		J. Invoice Number		
K. Instructions for Nondelivery				
K1. [ ] Discard K2. [ ] Return to Sender K3. [ ] Redirect				

1. In which box would you enter the number of pounds the package weighs?
   a. B
   b. C
   c. C1
   d. C2

2. What information belongs in box J?
   a. license number
   b. contents
   c. shipping type
   d. invoice number

3. In which box would you expect to find "Brazil"?
   a. D
   b. E
   c. F
   d. H

4. What information belongs in box E?
   a. value
   b. tariff code
   c. shipping type
   d. contents

5. Which box indicates priority shipping?
   a. F
   b. G1
   c. G2
   d. G3

6. If seven items are being sent, which box indicates this?
   a. A
   b. B
   c. C
   d. D

7. The license number "XJ786HU" belongs in which box?
   a. E
   b. H
   c. I
   d. J

8. If the package is worth $700, where would you include this information?
   a. box A
   b. box B
   c. box D
   d. box E

9. The invoice number is found in which box?
   a. H
   b. I
   c. J
   d. K

10. If the package(s) cannot be delivered, which box indicates what to do with the package(s)?
   a. D
   b. F
   c. G
   d. K

Mail Hold Request

A. First Name	B. Last Name

C. Address	

D. City	E. State	F. ZIP Code

G. Start Date	H. End Date

I. Signature	
	☐ 1. Please deliver held mail.
J. Date	☐ 2. I will pick up held mail.

11. You would expect to see "Las Vegas" in which box?
   a. C
   b. D
   c. E
   d. F

12. If a family will be away and not receiving mail from July 5 to September 8, which date would be written in box H?
   a. July 5
   b. July 5–September 8
   c. September 8
   d. July 8

13. Held mail will be delivered if which box is checked?
   a. A
   b. B
   c. 1
   d. 2

14. A signature belongs in which box?
   a. A
   b. B
   c. G
   d. I

15. Which of these would be an entry in box C?
   a. 5699 Main Street
   b. Jones
   c. 5/12/2009
   d. California

16. All of the following would complete box F EXCEPT
   a. 88409
   b. 4430
   c. 44130
   d. 82604

17. You would expect to find "California" in which of the following boxes?
   a. C
   b. D
   c. E
   d. F

18. The first day for the mail to be delivered is indicated in which box?
   a. G
   b. H
   c. J
   d. I

19. To indicate that mail will be picked up, which of the following boxes must be checked?

a. G

b. H

c. 1

d. 2

20. Which of these would be an entry in box F?

a. 29031

b. 2/9/2009

c. 29 31st Street

d. $29.31

Bulk Mailing Instructions

A. Item Type (check one)			
A1. [ ] Flyer	A2. [ ] Catalog	A3. [ ] Magazine	A4. [ ] Other

B. Delivery Zones (check all that apply)			
B1. [ ] 1 – 4	B2. [ ] 5 – 14	B3. [ ] 15 – 23	

C. Route Numbers (check one)			
C1. [ ] 67 – 93	C2. [ ] 108 – 171	C3. [ ] 197 – 231	C4. [ ] 371 – 530

Delivery Start Date			F. Postmark
D1. Mo.	D2. Day	D3. Year	
Delivery End Date			
D4. Mo.	D5. Day	D6. Year	

E. Other Delivery Instructions (check one)		
E1. [ ] One Time Delivery	E3. [ ] Monthly	
E2. [ ] Weekly	E4. [ ] Annually	G. Clerk's Signature

21. How many check marks should there be in box E?

a. 1

b. 2

c. 3

d. 4

22. If delivery should start on April 25, which line(s) would be filled in?

a. D1, D3

b. D4, D5

c. D1, D2

d. D5

23. If items are mailed in bulk only once, which box would be checked?

a. E1

b. E2

c. E3

d. E4

24. All of the following boxes require check marks EXCEPT

a. A

b. C

c. E

d. G

25. Which of the following would complete box C?
  a. month
  b. day
  c. check mark
  d. postmark

26. If delivery should end on May 10, 2009, what should be written in line D5?
  a. May
  b. 10
  c. 2009
  d. 5/10/2009

27. Which of the following would complete box G?
  a. postmark
  b. check mark
  c. date
  d. signature

28. If items are being shipped to zones 1–4 and 15–23, which boxes should be checked?
  a. B1 and B2
  b. B2 and B3
  c. B1 and B3
  d. B1 only

29. If the items being mailed are paperback books, which box should be checked?
  a. B1
  b. C2
  c. E
  d. A4

30. Which box requires a postmark?
  a. A
  b. E
  c. F
  d. G

Part C, Section 1—Coding

Directions: Read and review the **Coding Guide**. Each of the 36 questions offers an **Address**. Choose which **Delivery Route** each address belongs in according to the Coding Guide.

Time: 6 minutes

CODING GUIDE	
ADDRESS RANGE	**DELIVERY ROUTE**
99–199 Somerset Blvd 801–900 First Avenue	A
200–299 Somerset Blvd 901–1200 First Avenue 101–3400 Yosemite Street	B
15–30 Route 3 55–900 Broadway 3401–3700 Yosemite Street	C
All mail that doesn't belong in one of the address ranges listed here.	D

1. 150 Somerset Blvd
   a. Delivery Route A
   b. Delivery Route B
   c. Delivery Route C
   d. Delivery Route D

2. 3000 Yosemite Street
   a. Delivery Route A
   b. Delivery Route B
   c. Delivery Route C
   d. Delivery Route D

3. 15 Route 3
   a. Delivery Route A
   b. Delivery Route B
   c. Delivery Route C
   d. Delivery Route D

4. 100 Somerset Blvd
   a. Delivery Route A
   b. Delivery Route B
   c. Delivery Route C
   d. Delivery Route D

5. 800 First Avenue
   a. Delivery Route A
   b. Delivery Route B
   c. Delivery Route C
   d. Delivery Route D

6. 124 Sumerset Blvd
   a. Delivery Route A
   b. Delivery Route B
   c. Delivery Route C
   d. Delivery Route D

7. 65 Broadway
  a. Delivery Route A
  b. Delivery Route B
  c. Delivery Route C
  d. Delivery Route D

8. 198 Somerset Blvd
  a. Delivery Route A
  b. Delivery Route B
  c. Delivery Route C
  d. Delivery Route D

9. 3415 Yosemite Street
  a. Delivery Route A
  b. Delivery Route B
  c. Delivery Route C
  d. Delivery Route D

10. 874 First Drive
  a. Delivery Route A
  b. Delivery Route B
  c. Delivery Route C
  d. Delivery Route D

11. 201 Somerset Blvd
  a. Delivery Route A
  b. Delivery Route B
  c. Delivery Route C
  d. Delivery Route D

12. 1100 First Avenue
  a. Delivery Route A
  b. Delivery Route B
  c. Delivery Route C
  d. Delivery Route D

13. 27 Broadway
  a. Delivery Route A
  b. Delivery Route B
  c. Delivery Route C
  d. Delivery Route D

14. 27 Route 3
  a. Delivery Route A
  b. Delivery Route B
  c. Delivery Route C
  d. Delivery Route D

15. 3240 Yoseff Street
  a. Delivery Route A
  b. Delivery Route B
  c. Delivery Route C
  d. Delivery Route D

16. 201 Yosemite Street
  a. Delivery Route A
  b. Delivery Route B
  c. Delivery Route C
  d. Delivery Route D

17. 35 Route 3
  a. Delivery Route A
  b. Delivery Route B
  c. Delivery Route C
  d. Delivery Route D

18. 800 First Avenue
  a. Delivery Route A
  b. Delivery Route B
  c. Delivery Route C
  d. Delivery Route D

19. 34 Yosemite Rd
  a. Delivery Route A
  b. Delivery Route B
  c. Delivery Route C
  d. Delivery Route D

20. 700 Broadway
  a. Delivery Route A
  b. Delivery Route B
  c. Delivery Route C
  d. Delivery Route D

21. 1130 First Avenue
  a. Delivery Route A
  b. Delivery Route B
  c. Delivery Route C
  d. Delivery Route D

22. 270 Yosemite Street
  a. Delivery Route A
  b. Delivery Route B
  c. Delivery Route C
  d. Delivery Route D

23. 3402 Yosemite Street
  a. Delivery Route A
  b. Delivery Route B
  c. Delivery Route C
  d. Delivery Route D

24. 81 W Broadway
  a. Delivery Route A
  b. Delivery Route B
  c. Delivery Route C
  d. Delivery Route D

25. 18 Route 3
  a. Delivery Route A
  b. Delivery Route B
  c. Delivery Route C
  d. Delivery Route D

26. 105 Yosemite Street
  a. Delivery Route A
  b. Delivery Route B
  c. Delivery Route C
  d. Delivery Route D

27. 650 Broadway
  a. Delivery Route A
  b. Delivery Route B
  c. Delivery Route C
  d. Delivery Route D

28. 271 Somerset Blvd
  a. Delivery Route A
  b. Delivery Route B
  c. Delivery Route C
  d. Delivery Route D

29. 29 Route 3
  a. Delivery Route A
  b. Delivery Route B
  c. Delivery Route C
  d. Delivery Route D

30. 87 Yosemite Street
  a. Delivery Route A
  b. Delivery Route B
  c. Delivery Route C
  d. Delivery Route D

31. 930 Second Avenue
  a. Delivery Route A
  b. Delivery Route B
  c. Delivery Route C
  d. Delivery Route D

32. 15 Route 8
  a. Delivery Route A
  b. Delivery Route B
  c. Delivery Route C
  d. Delivery Route D

33. 864 Broad Street
  a. Delivery Route A
  b. Delivery Route B
  c. Delivery Route C
  d. Delivery Route D

34. 80 First Avenue
  a. Delivery Route A
  b. Delivery Route B
  c. Delivery Route C
  d. Delivery Route D

35. 3211 Yosemite Street
    a. Delivery Route A
    b. Delivery Route B
    c. Delivery Route C
    d. Delivery Route D

36. 101 Somerset Blvd
    a. Delivery Route A
    b. Delivery Route B
    c. Delivery Route C
    d. Delivery Route D

Part C, Section 2—Memory

Directions: Spend three minutes memorizing the information found in the Coding Guide. You may NOT take any notes during this time. Next, you will answer the 72 questions. Each question offers an **Address.** Choose which **Delivery Route** each address belongs in according to your memory of the Coding Guide. **Note: You may NOT turn back to the page displaying the Coding Guide once the Memory section has begun.**

Time: 3 minutes for memorization, 7 minutes to answer questions

CODING GUIDE	
ADDRESS RANGE	**DELIVERY ROUTE**
99–199 Somerset Blvd 801–900 First Avenue	A
200–299 Somerset Blvd 901–1200 First Avenue 101–3400 Yosemite Street	B
15–30 Route 3 55–900 Broadway 3401–3700 Yosemite Street	C
All mail that doesn't belong in one of the address ranges listed here.	D

37. 5 Broadway
   a. Delivery Route A
   b. Delivery Route B
   c. Delivery Route C
   d. Delivery Route D

38. 3544 Yosemite Street
   a. Delivery Route A
   b. Delivery Route B
   c. Delivery Route C
   d. Delivery Route D

39. 299 Somerset Blvd
   a. Delivery Route A
   b. Delivery Route B
   c. Delivery Route C
   d. Delivery Route D

40. 830 First Avenue
   a. Delivery Route A
   b. Delivery Route B
   c. Delivery Route C
   d. Delivery Route D

41. 18 Route 3
   a. Delivery Route A
   b. Delivery Route B
   c. Delivery Route C
   d. Delivery Route D

42. 81 First Avenue
   a. Delivery Route A
   b. Delivery Route B
   c. Delivery Route C
   d. Delivery Route D

43. 15 Route 3
   a. Delivery Route A
   b. Delivery Route B
   c. Delivery Route C
   d. Delivery Route D

44. 807 First Avenue
   a. Delivery Route A
   b. Delivery Route B
   c. Delivery Route C
   d. Delivery Route D

45. 289 Somerset Blvd
   a. Delivery Route A
   b. Delivery Route B
   c. Delivery Route C
   d. Delivery Route D

46. 135 Somerset Blvd
   a. Delivery Route A
   b. Delivery Route B
   c. Delivery Route C
   d. Delivery Route D

47. 1266 Yosemite Avenue
   a. Delivery Route A
   b. Delivery Route B
   c. Delivery Route C
   d. Delivery Route D

48. 187 Somerset Blvd
   a. Delivery Route A
   b. Delivery Route B
   c. Delivery Route C
   d. Delivery Route D

49. 30 Route 31
   a. Delivery Route A
   b. Delivery Route B
   c. Delivery Route C
   d. Delivery Route D

50. 780 Broadway
   a. Delivery Route A
   b. Delivery Route B
   c. Delivery Route C
   d. Delivery Route D

51. 820 First Avenue
  a. Delivery Route A
  b. Delivery Route B
  c. Delivery Route C
  d. Delivery Route D

52. 121 Somerset Blvd
  a. Delivery Route A
  b. Delivery Route B
  c. Delivery Route C
  d. Delivery Route D

53. 801 First Avenue
  a. Delivery Route A
  b. Delivery Route B
  c. Delivery Route C
  d. Delivery Route D

54. 1000 First Avenue
  a. Delivery Route A
  b. Delivery Route B
  c. Delivery Route C
  d. Delivery Route D

55. 16 Route 6
  a. Delivery Route A
  b. Delivery Route B
  c. Delivery Route C
  d. Delivery Route D

56. 175 Somerset Blvd
  a. Delivery Route A
  b. Delivery Route B
  c. Delivery Route C
  d. Delivery Route D

57. 21 Route 3
  a. Delivery Route A
  b. Delivery Route B
  c. Delivery Route C
  d. Delivery Route D

58. 120 Yosemite Street
  a. Delivery Route A
  b. Delivery Route B
  c. Delivery Route C
  d. Delivery Route D

59. 199 Somerset Blvd
  a. Delivery Route A
  b. Delivery Route B
  c. Delivery Route C
  d. Delivery Route D

60. 1030 First Avenue
  a. Delivery Route A
  b. Delivery Route B
  c. Delivery Route C
  d. Delivery Route D

61. 899 First Avenue
  a. Delivery Route A
  b. Delivery Route B
  c. Delivery Route C
  d. Delivery Route D

62. 1199 First Avenue
  a. Delivery Route A
  b. Delivery Route B
  c. Delivery Route C
  d. Delivery Route D

63. 109 Somerset Blvd
  a. Delivery Route A
  b. Delivery Route B
  c. Delivery Route C
  d. Delivery Route D

64. 3511 Yosemite Street
  a. Delivery Route A
  b. Delivery Route B
  c. Delivery Route C
  d. Delivery Route D

65. 733 Broad Road
   a. Delivery Route A
   b. Delivery Route B
   c. Delivery Route C
   d. Delivery Route D

66. 278 Somerset Blvd
   a. Delivery Route A
   b. Delivery Route B
   c. Delivery Route C
   d. Delivery Route D

67. 15 Route 5
   a. Delivery Route A
   b. Delivery Route B
   c. Delivery Route C
   d. Delivery Route D

68. 866 First Avenue
   a. Delivery Route A
   b. Delivery Route B
   c. Delivery Route C
   d. Delivery Route D

69. 22 Route 3
   a. Delivery Route A
   b. Delivery Route B
   c. Delivery Route C
   d. Delivery Route D

70. 883 Broadway
   a. Delivery Route A
   b. Delivery Route B
   c. Delivery Route C
   d. Delivery Route D

71. 102 Yosemite Street
   a. Delivery Route A
   b. Delivery Route B
   c. Delivery Route C
   d. Delivery Route D

72. 111 Somerset Blvd
   a. Delivery Route A
   b. Delivery Route B
   c. Delivery Route C
   d. Delivery Route D

▶ Answers

Part A—Address Checking

1. d.	**16.** d.	**31.** c.	**46.** c.
2. c.	**17.** b.	**32.** b.	**47.** d.
3. d.	**18.** c.	**33.** d.	**48.** a.
4. a.	**19.** c.	**34.** b.	**49.** d.
5. d.	**20.** a.	**35.** c.	**50.** d.
6. a.	**21.** d.	**36.** d.	**51.** b.
7. b.	**22.** b.	**37.** c.	**52.** a.
8. b.	**23.** c.	**38.** b.	**53.** c.
9. a.	**24.** a.	**39.** d.	**54.** b.
10. c.	**25.** b.	**40.** d.	**55.** b.
11. d.	**26.** d.	**41.** d.	**56.** c.
12. c.	**27.** b.	**42.** b.	**57.** b.
13. b.	**28.** b.	**43.** c.	**58.** c.
14. b.	**29.** b.	**44.** b.	**59.** d.
15. c.	**30.** d.	**45.** a.	**60.** d.

Part B—Forms Completion

1. c. Box C indicates weight. However, this box is divided into two other boxes to differentiate between pounds and ounces. Since the question asks for pounds, the information would be entered into box C1.

2. d. The invoice number is found in box J.

3. c. Only box F requires the name of a country, so **c** is correct.

4. b. The tariff code is found in box E.

5. b. Box G1 indicates priority shipping.

6. b. Seven is the quantity being sent; therefore, this information is found in box B.

7. c. License numbers belong in box I.

8. c. The value of the package is found in box D.

9. c. The invoice number is found in box J.

10. d. Box K includes the instruction for nondelivery. Choice **d** is the correct answer.

11. b. Box D requires a city, so **b** is correct.

12. c. The family is returning on September 8 and would pick up mail after that.

13. c. Box 1 reads, "Please deliver held mail."

14. d. The signature belongs in box I.

15. a. Box C should contain an address; therefore, **a** is correct.

16. b. Box F must have a standard, five digit ZIP code.

17. c. The name of a state belongs in box E.

18. a. Mail will be held from the start date that is indicated in box G.

19. d. Checking box 2 would indicate that held mail will be picked up.

20. a. Box F should contain a ZIP code; therefore, **a** is correct.

21. a. Box E includes instructions that read "check one"; therefore, **a** is the correct answer.

22. c. The month and day that delivery should start are found in D1 and D2.

23. a. Box E1 reads, "One-Time delivery"; therefore, **a** is correct.

24. d. Box G requires a signature, not a check mark.

25. c. The instructions in box C read, "check one"; therefore, a check mark is required.

26. b. Line D2 requires the day that delivery should start. The correct answer is 10.

27. d. Box G requires the clerk's signature.

28. c. Boxes B1 and B3 indicate delivery zones 1–4 and 15–23.

29. d. There are four item types listed in box A: flyer, catalog, magazine, and other. Since paperback books are not flyers, catalogs, or magazines, box A4 should be checked.

30. c. The postmark belongs in box F.

1. a.	**10.** d.	**19.** d.	**28.** b.
2. b.	**11.** b.	**20.** c.	**29.** c.
3. c.	**12.** b.	**21.** b.	**30.** d.
4. a.	**13.** d.	**22.** b.	**31.** d.
5. d.	**14.** c.	**23.** c.	**32.** d.
6. d.	**15.** d.	**24.** d.	**33.** d.
7. c.	**16.** b.	**25.** c.	**34.** d.
8. a.	**17.** d.	**26.** b.	**35.** b.
9. c.	**18.** d.	**27.** c.	**36.** a.

Part C, Section 1—Coding

Part C, Section 2—Memory

37. d.	**46.** a.	**55.** d.	**64.** c.
38. c.	**47.** d.	**56.** a.	**65.** d.
39. b.	**48.** a.	**57.** c.	**66.** b.
40. a.	**49.** d.	**58.** b.	**67.** d.
41. c.	**50.** c.	**59.** a.	**68.** a.
42. d.	**51.** a.	**60.** b.	**69.** c.
43. c.	**52.** a.	**61.** a.	**70.** c.
44. a.	**53.** a.	**62.** b.	**71.** b.
45. b.	**54.** b.	**63.** a.	**72.** a.

▶ Scoring

As with the first exam in this book, first you must determine your raw score on the exam.

Your Raw Score

Here's how to determine your raw score for each part.

Part A—Address Checking

First, count the questions you got right. Then, count the number of questions you got wrong. Questions you didn't answer don't count either way. Don't forget to multiply the questions you got wrong by $\frac{1}{3}$.

1. Number of questions right: _____
2. Number of questions wrong: _____
3. Number of questions wrong multiply by $\frac{1}{3}$: _____
4. Subtract number 3 from number 1: _____

The result in line 4 is your raw score on Part A.

Part B—Forms Completion

Count the questions you got right. Questions you got wrong or didn't answer don't count either way.

Number of questions right: _____

The result is your raw score on Part B.

Part C, Section 1—Coding

First, count the questions you got right. Then, count the number of questions you got wrong. Questions you didn't answer don't count either way. Don't forget to multiply the questions you got wrong by $\frac{1}{3}$.

1. Number of questions right: _____
2. Number of questions wrong: _____
3. Number of questions wrong multiplied by $\frac{1}{3}$: _____
4. Subtract number 3 from number 1: _____

The result in line 4 is your raw score on this section of Part C.

Part C, Section 2—Memory

First, count the questions you got right. Then, count the number of questions you got wrong. Questions you didn't answer don't count either way. Don't forget to multiply the questions you got wrong by $\frac{1}{3}$.

1. Number of questions right: _____
2. Number of questions wrong: _____
3. Number of questions wrong multiplied by $\frac{1}{3}$: _____
4. Subtract number 3 from number 1: _____

The result in line 4 is your raw score on this section of Part C.

Part D—Personal Characteristics and Experience Inventory

Remember, there are no right or wrong answers on this section of Test 473 and these questions appear only once in Chapter 8. In addition, the USPS has not released information on how your responses to the questions are "scored." For these reasons, Part D is not used to calculate your raw score on this practice exam.

Total Raw Score

For your total raw score, add together the four raw scores you just calculated.

Total raw score: _____

Basic Rating

To calculate your basic rating, the USPS converts your raw scores on Parts A, B, and C and factors in the results of Part D. As aforementioned, the basic rating is based on a scale of 1 to 100 with 70 being the required passing score to be eligible for a job with the USPS. It is very difficult to give you an accurate basic rating based on this practice exam; however, if your raw score is above 100, you are on your way to passing the official exam.

The Next Step

Chances are you've seen some improvement—maybe a lot of improvement—since you took the first exam in this book. If you're still weak in some areas, continue to review the relevant chapters before you take the next practice exam.

10 ▶ Practice Postal Worker Exam 3

CHAPTER SUMMARY

This is the third practice exam in this book based on Test 473, the Postal Worker Exam. This test provides even more practice to help you get ready for test day.

Take this exam when you've worked through the chapters on the various sections of the exam. Remember, to practice Part D—Personal Characteristics and Experience Inventory—review Chapter 8, as these questions do not appear in this practice exam.

Before you start this test, prepare to simulate the actual test-taking experience as much as possible. Get out your stopwatch or alarm clock so that you can time yourself on each part of the test.

The only other things you need before you begin the test are a quiet place to work, some No. 2 pencils, and enough time to complete the test at one sitting—about an hour, with a couple of minutes for a break between each part.

The answer sheet you should use for answering the questions is on pages 143–144. Then comes the exam itself, and after that is the answer key. The answer key is followed by a section on how to score your exam.

▶ Part A: Address Checking

1.	ⓐ	ⓑ	ⓒ	ⓓ	21.	ⓐ	ⓑ	ⓒ	ⓓ	41.	ⓐ	ⓑ	ⓒ	ⓓ
2.	ⓐ	ⓑ	ⓒ	ⓓ	22.	ⓐ	ⓑ	ⓒ	ⓓ	42.	ⓐ	ⓑ	ⓒ	ⓓ
3.	ⓐ	ⓑ	ⓒ	ⓓ	23.	ⓐ	ⓑ	ⓒ	ⓓ	43.	ⓐ	ⓑ	ⓒ	ⓓ
4.	ⓐ	ⓑ	ⓒ	ⓓ	24.	ⓐ	ⓑ	ⓒ	ⓓ	44.	ⓐ	ⓑ	ⓒ	ⓓ
5.	ⓐ	ⓑ	ⓒ	ⓓ	25.	ⓐ	ⓑ	ⓒ	ⓓ	45.	ⓐ	ⓑ	ⓒ	ⓓ
6.	ⓐ	ⓑ	ⓒ	ⓓ	26.	ⓐ	ⓑ	ⓒ	ⓓ	46.	ⓐ	ⓑ	ⓒ	ⓓ
7.	ⓐ	ⓑ	ⓒ	ⓓ	27.	ⓐ	ⓑ	ⓒ	ⓓ	47.	ⓐ	ⓑ	ⓒ	ⓓ
8.	ⓐ	ⓑ	ⓒ	ⓓ	28.	ⓐ	ⓑ	ⓒ	ⓓ	48.	ⓐ	ⓑ	ⓒ	ⓓ
9.	ⓐ	ⓑ	ⓒ	ⓓ	29.	ⓐ	ⓑ	ⓒ	ⓓ	49.	ⓐ	ⓑ	ⓒ	ⓓ
10.	ⓐ	ⓑ	ⓒ	ⓓ	30.	ⓐ	ⓑ	ⓒ	ⓓ	50.	ⓐ	ⓑ	ⓒ	ⓓ
11.	ⓐ	ⓑ	ⓒ	ⓓ	31.	ⓐ	ⓑ	ⓒ	ⓓ	51.	ⓐ	ⓑ	ⓒ	ⓓ
12.	ⓐ	ⓑ	ⓒ	ⓓ	32.	ⓐ	ⓑ	ⓒ	ⓓ	52.	ⓐ	ⓑ	ⓒ	ⓓ
13.	ⓐ	ⓑ	ⓒ	ⓓ	33.	ⓐ	ⓑ	ⓒ	ⓓ	53.	ⓐ	ⓑ	ⓒ	ⓓ
14.	ⓐ	ⓑ	ⓒ	ⓓ	34.	ⓐ	ⓑ	ⓒ	ⓓ	54.	ⓐ	ⓑ	ⓒ	ⓓ
15.	ⓐ	ⓑ	ⓒ	ⓓ	35.	ⓐ	ⓑ	ⓒ	ⓓ	55.	ⓐ	ⓑ	ⓒ	ⓓ
16.	ⓐ	ⓑ	ⓒ	ⓓ	36.	ⓐ	ⓑ	ⓒ	ⓓ	56.	ⓐ	ⓑ	ⓒ	ⓓ
17.	ⓐ	ⓑ	ⓒ	ⓓ	37.	ⓐ	ⓑ	ⓒ	ⓓ	57.	ⓐ	ⓑ	ⓒ	ⓓ
18.	ⓐ	ⓑ	ⓒ	ⓓ	38.	ⓐ	ⓑ	ⓒ	ⓓ	58.	ⓐ	ⓑ	ⓒ	ⓓ
19.	ⓐ	ⓑ	ⓒ	ⓓ	39.	ⓐ	ⓑ	ⓒ	ⓓ	59.	ⓐ	ⓑ	ⓒ	ⓓ
20.	ⓐ	ⓑ	ⓒ	ⓓ	40.	ⓐ	ⓑ	ⓒ	ⓓ	60.	ⓐ	ⓑ	ⓒ	ⓓ

▶ Part B: Forms Completion

1.	ⓐ	ⓑ	ⓒ	ⓓ	11.	ⓐ	ⓑ	ⓒ	ⓓ	21.	ⓐ	ⓑ	ⓒ	ⓓ
2.	ⓐ	ⓑ	ⓒ	ⓓ	12.	ⓐ	ⓑ	ⓒ	ⓓ	22.	ⓐ	ⓑ	ⓒ	ⓓ
3.	ⓐ	ⓑ	ⓒ	ⓓ	13.	ⓐ	ⓑ	ⓒ	ⓓ	23.	ⓐ	ⓑ	ⓒ	ⓓ
4.	ⓐ	ⓑ	ⓒ	ⓓ	14.	ⓐ	ⓑ	ⓒ	ⓓ	24.	ⓐ	ⓑ	ⓒ	ⓓ
5.	ⓐ	ⓑ	ⓒ	ⓓ	15.	ⓐ	ⓑ	ⓒ	ⓓ	25.	ⓐ	ⓑ	ⓒ	ⓓ
6.	ⓐ	ⓑ	ⓒ	ⓓ	16.	ⓐ	ⓑ	ⓒ	ⓓ	26.	ⓐ	ⓑ	ⓒ	ⓓ
7.	ⓐ	ⓑ	ⓒ	ⓓ	17.	ⓐ	ⓑ	ⓒ	ⓓ	27.	ⓐ	ⓑ	ⓒ	ⓓ
8.	ⓐ	ⓑ	ⓒ	ⓓ	18.	ⓐ	ⓑ	ⓒ	ⓓ	28.	ⓐ	ⓑ	ⓒ	ⓓ
9.	ⓐ	ⓑ	ⓒ	ⓓ	19.	ⓐ	ⓑ	ⓒ	ⓓ	29.	ⓐ	ⓑ	ⓒ	ⓓ
10.	ⓐ	ⓑ	ⓒ	ⓓ	20.	ⓐ	ⓑ	ⓒ	ⓓ	30.	ⓐ	ⓑ	ⓒ	ⓓ

▶ Part C: Section 1–Coding

1. ⓐ ⓑ ⓒ ⓓ
2. ⓐ ⓑ ⓒ ⓓ
3. ⓐ ⓑ ⓒ ⓓ
4. ⓐ ⓑ ⓒ ⓓ
5. ⓐ ⓑ ⓒ ⓓ
6. ⓐ ⓑ ⓒ ⓓ
7. ⓐ ⓑ ⓒ ⓓ
8. ⓐ ⓑ ⓒ ⓓ
9. ⓐ ⓑ ⓒ ⓓ
10. ⓐ ⓑ ⓒ ⓓ
11. ⓐ ⓑ ⓒ ⓓ
12. ⓐ ⓑ ⓒ ⓓ
13. ⓐ ⓑ ⓒ ⓓ
14. ⓐ ⓑ ⓒ ⓓ
15. ⓐ ⓑ ⓒ ⓓ
16. ⓐ ⓑ ⓒ ⓓ
17. ⓐ ⓑ ⓒ ⓓ
18. ⓐ ⓑ ⓒ ⓓ
19. ⓐ ⓑ ⓒ ⓓ
20. ⓐ ⓑ ⓒ ⓓ
21. ⓐ ⓑ ⓒ ⓓ
22. ⓐ ⓑ ⓒ ⓓ
23. ⓐ ⓑ ⓒ ⓓ
24. ⓐ ⓑ ⓒ ⓓ
25. ⓐ ⓑ ⓒ ⓓ
26. ⓐ ⓑ ⓒ ⓓ
27. ⓐ ⓑ ⓒ ⓓ
28. ⓐ ⓑ ⓒ ⓓ
29. ⓐ ⓑ ⓒ ⓓ
30. ⓐ ⓑ ⓒ ⓓ
31. ⓐ ⓑ ⓒ ⓓ
32. ⓐ ⓑ ⓒ ⓓ
33. ⓐ ⓑ ⓒ ⓓ
34. ⓐ ⓑ ⓒ ⓓ
35. ⓐ ⓑ ⓒ ⓓ
36. ⓐ ⓑ ⓒ ⓓ

▶ Part C: Section 2–Memory

37. ⓐ ⓑ ⓒ ⓓ
38. ⓐ ⓑ ⓒ ⓓ
39. ⓐ ⓑ ⓒ ⓓ
40. ⓐ ⓑ ⓒ ⓓ
41. ⓐ ⓑ ⓒ ⓓ
42. ⓐ ⓑ ⓒ ⓓ
43. ⓐ ⓑ ⓒ ⓓ
44. ⓐ ⓑ ⓒ ⓓ
45. ⓐ ⓑ ⓒ ⓓ
46. ⓐ ⓑ ⓒ ⓓ
47. ⓐ ⓑ ⓒ ⓓ
48. ⓐ ⓑ ⓒ ⓓ
49. ⓐ ⓑ ⓒ ⓓ
50. ⓐ ⓑ ⓒ ⓓ
51. ⓐ ⓑ ⓒ ⓓ
52. ⓐ ⓑ ⓒ ⓓ
53. ⓐ ⓑ ⓒ ⓓ
54. ⓐ ⓑ ⓒ ⓓ
55. ⓐ ⓑ ⓒ ⓓ
56. ⓐ ⓑ ⓒ ⓓ
57. ⓐ ⓑ ⓒ ⓓ
58. ⓐ ⓑ ⓒ ⓓ
59. ⓐ ⓑ ⓒ ⓓ
60. ⓐ ⓑ ⓒ ⓓ
61. ⓐ ⓑ ⓒ ⓓ
62. ⓐ ⓑ ⓒ ⓓ
63. ⓐ ⓑ ⓒ ⓓ
64. ⓐ ⓑ ⓒ ⓓ
65. ⓐ ⓑ ⓒ ⓓ
66. ⓐ ⓑ ⓒ ⓓ
67. ⓐ ⓑ ⓒ ⓓ
68. ⓐ ⓑ ⓒ ⓓ
69. ⓐ ⓑ ⓒ ⓓ
70. ⓐ ⓑ ⓒ ⓓ
71. ⓐ ⓑ ⓒ ⓓ
72. ⓐ ⓑ ⓒ ⓓ

▶ Practice Postal Worker Exam 3

Part A—Address Checking

Directions: Review and compare the information in the **List to Be Checked** with the information in the **Correct List**. To answer each question, you must decide if there are **No errors** (**a**), an error in the **Address only** (**b**), an error in the **ZIP code only** (**c**), or an error in **Both** (**d**) the address and the ZIP code. This part has 60 questions.

Time: 11 minutes

	CORRECT LIST		LIST TO BE CHECKED	
QUESTION	**ADDRESS**	**ZIP CODE**	**ADDRESS**	**ZIP CODE**
1.	6754 Boston Ln Neoga, IL	62477-5433	6754 Boston Ln Neoga, IN	62477-5433
2.	543 Hillman Dr Soap Lake, WA	98851	543 Hillman Dr Soap Lake, WA	98851
3.	9988 Gotry St Tacna, AZ	85352	9988 Gotry Dr Tacna, AZ	85352
4.	7843 Junson Dr Summer Shade, KY	42166	7843 Junson Dr Summer Shade, KY	42116
5.	90001 Remin Road Mabie, WV	26278-0877	9000 Remin Road Mabie, WV	26278-0877
6.	213 W 17th Street Elihu, KY	42501	213 W 7th Street Elihu, KY	42001
7.	876 Yosemite Ave Astoria, NY	11105	867 Yosemite Ave Astoria, NY	11005
8.	9054 Thompson Street Des Arc, MO	63636-9378	9054 Thomson Street Des Arc, MO	63636-9738
9.	3425 Greene Cir Delight, AR	71940	3425 Greene Cir Delight, AR	79140
10.	6547 Grand Avenue Lyon, MS	38645	6547 Grant Avenue Lions, MS	36845
11.	564 Wilkinson Dr Lovejoy, GA	30250	564 Wilkins Dr Lovejoy, GA	30200

a. No errors
b. Address only
c. ZIP code only
d. Both

	CORRECT LIST		LIST TO BE CHECKED	
QUESTION	ADDRESS	ZIP CODE	ADDRESS	ZIP CODE
12.	8976 Saivan St Del Rey, CA	93616	8976 Saivan St Del Rey, CA	93616
13.	4355 Yuma Ave Lodi, NJ	07644	435 Yuma Ave Lodi, NJ	07464
14.	3232 Upas St Mesa, WA	99343-1453	3232 Upas St Mesa, WI	99343-1453
15.	768 E 27th Street Paragon, IN	46166-4582	768 E 27th Street Paragon, IN	46166-4582
16.	2765 Hema Cir Talent, OR	97540	2765 Herma Cir Talent, OR	97440
17.	3245 Keer Way Kapolei, HI	96707-2346	3254 Keer Way Kapolei, HI	96707-2346
18.	546 Johnston Way Anchorage, AK	99599	546 Johnston Way Anchorage, AL	99959
19.	1243 8th Ave Cushing, IA	51018	1243 6th Ave Cushing, IA	50118
20.	777 40th Street Hiles, WI	54511	777 40th Street Hiles, WI	54511
21.	PO Box 89754 Merom, IN	47861	PO Box 89754 Merom, IN	47681
22.	3113 Leitz Boulevard Rocky, OK	73661	3113 Letz Boulevard Rocky, OK	73661
23.	8653 Bates St Sod, WV	25564-3463	8653 Bates St Sod, WV	25564-3463
24.	9888 Ian Boulevard Fort Yates, ND	58538	9888 Ian Boulevard Fort Yount, ND	58358
25.	67 Murray Ave Bay Pines, FL	33744	67 Murray Ave Bay Pines, FL	33444
26.	9099 Dennison Street Chaska, MN	55318-2344	9099 Denniso Street Chaska, MN	55318-2344

a. No errors
b. Address only
c. ZIP code only
d. Both

	CORRECT LIST		LIST TO BE CHECKED	
QUESTION	ADDRESS	ZIP CODE	ADDRESS	ZIP CODE
27.	665 Meredith Ln Cecil, PA	15321	65 Meredith Ln Cecil, PA	15312
28.	7533 Caesar Street George West, TX	78022	7533 Caesar Street George West, TX	78022
29.	8716 Bell Lane Ivy, VA	22945-2901	8716 Bell Lane Ivy, VA	22945-2901
30.	4366 Centra St Norwood, CO	81423	4366 Centra St Norwood, CO	81423
31.	8888 Highway 38 Jarvis, KY	40906	8888 Highway 38 Jarvis, KY	40996
32.	2141 Hilltop Dr Dogpatch, AR	72648	2441 Hilltop Dr Dogpatch, AR	72648
33.	3498 Pacific Way Mayo, MD	21106	3498 Pacific Highway Mayo, MD	20106
34.	7761 Jory Road Cassel, CA	96016	7761 Jory Drive Cassel, CA	96016
35.	913 Zappone Dr Alger, OH	45812-3466	913 Zappone Dr Alger, OH	45812-3646
36.	PO Box 23496 Colts Neck, NJ	07722-1572	PO Box 23496 Colts Neck, ND	07722-1572
37.	91 Third Ave New York, NY	10002	91 Third Ave New York, NY	10012
38.	3331 Rohen Dr Bessie, OK	73622	3331 Rohen Dr Bessie, OK	73622
39.	3322 Tate St Bimble, KY	40915-2473	3322 Tate St Bumble, KY	40915-2743
40.	3967 Saunders Road Fairton, NJ	08320	3967 Saunders Road Fair lawn, NJ	80320
41.	89 First Avenue Etta, MS	38627	89 First Avenue Etta, MS	38627

a. No errors
b. Address only
c. ZIP code only
d. Both

	CORRECT LIST		LIST TO BE CHECKED	
QUESTION	ADDRESS	ZIP CODE	ADDRESS	ZIP CODE
42.	2211 Chaffee Boulevard Geff, IL	62842	2211 Chaffee Boulevard Geffin, IL	62832
43.	7632 Jergen Street Lock Haven, PA	17745	7632 Jergen Street Lock Haven, PA	17475
44.	PO Box 60182 Milville, DE	19967-2364	PO Box 182 Milville, DE	19667-2364
45.	9961 Milden Avenue Peralta, NM	87042	9961 Milden Avenue Peralta, NM	78042
46.	76 Fourth Ave W Saint Mary, MT	59417	76 Fourth Ave W Saint Mary, MI	59417
47.	87 Elson Boulevard Sylvania, AL	35988	87 Ellison Boulevard Sylvania, AL	35988
48.	23 83rd St Mineral, WA	98355	23 W 83rd St Mineral, WA	98355
49.	881 Deventer Boulevard Oak Forest, IL	60452-3571	881 Deventer Boulevard Oak Forest, IA	60422-3571
50.	2134 April Avenue Sage, AR	72573	3134 April Avenue Sage, AR	72573
51.	6411 Marston St Lemhi, ID	83465	6411 Marston St Lemhi, ID	83465
52.	8854 Saratoga Dr Cardin, OK	74335	8854 Saratoga Dr Cardin, OK	73335
53.	7834 Roseboro Way Atka, AK	99547-2473	7834 Roseboro Way Atka, AZ	99547-2473
54.	1456 Churchill Boulevard Fisk, MO	63940	1456 Churchill Boulevard Fisk, MN	36940
55.	6711 Yoli Street Avalon, CA	90704	6711 Yoli Street Avalon, CA	97704
56.	1121 Homeny Cir Flatonia, TX	78941	1121 Homeny Cir Flatonia, TX	78941

a. No errors

b. Address only

c. ZIP code only

d. Both

		CORRECT LIST		LIST TO BE CHECKED	
QUESTION		**ADDRESS**	**ZIP CODE**	**ADDRESS**	**ZIP CODE**
57.		9734 Kirk Street Lame Deer, MT	59043-3576	9734 Kirk Street Lame Deer, MN	59043-3756
58.		PO Box 09456 Coatopa, AL	35470	PO Box 09456 Coatopa, AL	35470
59.		8789 Cherokee Way Joice, IA	50446	8789 Cherokee Way Joice, IA	54046
60.		6754 Timo Circle Milroy, IN	46156	6754 Timo Circle Milroy, IL	46156

a. No errors
b. Address only
c. ZIP code only
d. Both

Part B—Forms Completion

Directions: Review each form and answer the 30 questions that follow.

Time: 15 minutes

Address Change Form

1. Client Type 1A. [ ] Single Person 1B. [ ] Family 1C. [ ] Business		A1. Zone
2. Start Date		A2. Route Number
3. End Date		A3. Clerk's Name
4. Business Name (if applicable)		A4. Clerk's Signature
5. Last Name		A5. Expiration Date
6. First Name		A6. Postmark
7. Current Address		
7A. Current City	7B. Current State	7C. Current ZIP Code	
8. New Address		A7. Client Signature
8A. New City	8B. New State	8C. New ZIP Code	

1. How many ZIP codes are required to complete this form?
   a. 1
   b. 2
   c. 3
   d. 0

2. Which of the following would complete box A5?
   a. check mark
   b. signature
   c. postmark
   d. date

3. Which box would be checked if the Gleason company were moving to a new address?
   a. 1C
   b. 5
   c. 8
   d. A7

4. The street where the client currently lives would be found in which box?
   a. 7
   b. 7A
   c. 7B
   d. 7C

5. Box 4 should be completed if
    a. there is a check mark in 1A.
    b. there is a check mark in 1B.
    c. there is a check mark in 1C.
    d. the address is in Zone 1C.

6. In which two boxes could you find the clerk's name?
    a. A4 and A5
    b. A3 and A4
    c. A3 and A7
    d. A6 and A7

7. Which of the following boxes doesn't require dates?
    a. 2
    b. 3
    c. 4
    d. A5

8. "Wisconsin" would be an acceptable entry for
    a. box 7B only
    b. box 8B only
    c. box A1 only
    d. boxes 7B and 8B

9. Which of the following would be an acceptable entry for box 8C?
    a. Laramie
    b. 42343
    c. 4/23/09
    d. Wyoming

10. You could enter a name (first, last, full, or business) in all of the following EXCEPT
    a. A3
    b. 5
    c. 6
    d. 7

International Mail Receipt

1. Item Type (check one)		
1A. [ ] Letter 1B. [ ] Package		
2. Insurance Value $		
3. Recipient's Full Name		
3a. Address		
3b. City	3c. Postal Code	3d. Country
4. Item Delivered 4a. [ ] Yes 4b. [ ] No		5. Date Delivered 5a. Mo 5b. Day 5c. Year
6. Signature		6a. Date
7. Postmark		

11. Which of the following is an acceptable entry for box 2?
a. $11.83
b. 11783
c. 11/7/09
d. 11 83rd Street

12. How many boxes require a check mark?
a. 0
b. 1
c. 2
d. 3

13. Which of the following would be an appropriate entry for box 3d?
a. Buenos Aires
b. 86094
c. Canada
d. Arizona

14. If an item has not been delivered, which box would be checked?
a. A
b. 4a
c. B
d. 4b

15. Which two boxes include names?
a. 3 and 3a
b. 3 and 6
c. 6 and 6a
d. 6 and 7

16. How many dates would complete this receipt?
a. 0
b. 1
c. 2
d. 3

17. "Scotland" would complete which box?
   a. 3a
   b. 3d
   c. 3c
   d. 7

18. If a package is shipped to Mexico, what box should include a check mark?
   a. 1A
   b. 1B
   c. 4a
   d. 4b

19. If an item is delivered on February 13, 2009, what should appear in line 5b?
   a. February
   b. 13
   c. 2009
   d. 2/13/09

20. The postmark belongs in which box?
   a. 3c
   b. 1
   c. 6a
   d. 7

Confirmation of Delivery

A. Recipient's Name			
B. Recipient's Address	B1. City	B2. State	B3. ZIP Code
C. Article Description (check all that apply) C1. [　] Under 5 lbs　　C2. [　] Over 5 lbs　　C3. [　] Envelope　　C4. [　] Box			
D. Date			
E. Postmark	G. Service Requested (check one)		
	G1. Priority　　[　]		
	G2. Express　　[　]		
F. Confirmation Number	G3. Bulk Rate　　[　]		
	G4. Other　　[　]		

21. In which box would "California" be an appropriate entry?
   a. B
   b. B1
   c. B2
   d. B3

22. What would complete box D?
   a. postmark
   b. check mark
   c. confirmation number
   d. date

23. If magazines are sent bulk rate, which box should be checked?
a. G1
b. G2
c. G3
d. G4

24. Which of the following is a correct entry for box B2?
a. Newark
b. Rhode Island
c. San Francisco
d. Las Vegas

25. How many names should appear on this completed form?
a. 0
b. 1
c. 2
d. 3

26. If the delivery confirmation number is X8YZ7, where does it belong?
a. D
b. E
c. F
d. G

27. How many check marks should there be in box G?
a. 0
b. 1
c. 2
d. as many as apply

28. Which of the following would complete box B3?
a. 83201
b. 8320
c. 8/23/2009
d. Alaska

29. The postmark belongs in which box?
a. C
b. D
c. E
d. F

30. Which boxes should be checked if an envelope weighing two pounds is delivered?
a. C1 and C2
b. C2 and C3
c. C1 and C4
d. C1 and C3

Part C, Section 1—Coding

Directions: Read and review the **Coding Guide**. Each of the 26 questions offers an **Address**. Choose which **Delivery Route** each address belongs in according to the Coding Guide.

Time: 6 minutes

CODING GUIDE	
ADDRESS RANGE	**DELIVERY ROUTE**
700–1300 Jewell Street 1–70 Poway Road 401–600 Noyes Ave	A
201–800 Kettner Drive 99–400 C Street 601–2000 Noyes Ave	B
801–1100 Kettner Drive 499–700 C Street	C
All mail that doesn't belong in one of the address ranges listed here.	D

1. 760 Jewell Street
   a. Delivery Route A
   b. Delivery Route B
   c. Delivery Route C
   d. Delivery Route D

2. 444 Noyes Ave
   a. Delivery Route A
   b. Delivery Route B
   c. Delivery Route C
   d. Delivery Route D

3. 540 C Avenue
   a. Delivery Route A
   b. Delivery Route B
   c. Delivery Route C
   d. Delivery Route D

4. 222 Kettner Drive
   a. Delivery Route A
   b. Delivery Route B
   c. Delivery Route C
   d. Delivery Route D

5. 330 C Street
   a. Delivery Route A
   b. Delivery Route B
   c. Delivery Route C
   d. Delivery Route D

6. 523 C Street
   a. Delivery Route A
   b. Delivery Route B
   c. Delivery Route C
   d. Delivery Route D

7. 101 Kettner Drive
   a. Delivery Route A
   b. Delivery Route B
   c. Delivery Route C
   d. Delivery Route D

8. 67 Poway Road
   a. Delivery Route A
   b. Delivery Route B
   c. Delivery Route C
   d. Delivery Route D

9. 1200 Noyes Ave
   a. Delivery Route A
   b. Delivery Route B
   c. Delivery Route C
   d. Delivery Route D

10. 1001 Kettner Drive
   a. Delivery Route A
   b. Delivery Route B
   c. Delivery Route C
   d. Delivery Route D

11. 1450 Jewell Street
   a. Delivery Route A
   b. Delivery Route B
   c. Delivery Route C
   d. Delivery Route D

12. 1250 Jewell Street
   a. Delivery Route A
   b. Delivery Route B
   c. Delivery Route C
   d. Delivery Route D

13. 967 Kettner Drive
   a. Delivery Route A
   b. Delivery Route B
   c. Delivery Route C
   d. Delivery Route D

14. 321 C Street
   a. Delivery Route A
   b. Delivery Route B
   c. Delivery Route C
   d. Delivery Route D

15. 63 Poway Drive
   a. Delivery Route A
   b. Delivery Route B
   c. Delivery Route C
   d. Delivery Route D

16. 101 Poway Road
   a. Delivery Route A
   b. Delivery Route B
   c. Delivery Route C
   d. Delivery Route D

17. 687 C Street
   a. Delivery Route A
   b. Delivery Route B
   c. Delivery Route C
   d. Delivery Route D

18. 690 Noyes Ave
   a. Delivery Route A
   b. Delivery Route B
   c. Delivery Route C
   d. Delivery Route D

19. 478 Noyes Ave
   a. Delivery Route A
   b. Delivery Route B
   c. Delivery Route C
   d. Delivery Route D

20. 1089 Kettner Drive
   a. Delivery Route A
   b. Delivery Route B
   c. Delivery Route C
   d. Delivery Route D

21. 601 C Street
   a. Delivery Route A
   b. Delivery Route B
   c. Delivery Route C
   d. Delivery Route D

22. 533 Boyes Ave
   a. Delivery Route A
   b. Delivery Route B
   c. Delivery Route C
   d. Delivery Route D

23. 880 Jewell Street
  a. Delivery Route A
  b. Delivery Route B
  c. Delivery Route C
  d. Delivery Route D

24. 770 Kettner Drive
  a. Delivery Route A
  b. Delivery Route B
  c. Delivery Route C
  d. Delivery Route D

25. 131 Kettner Drive
  a. Delivery Route A
  b. Delivery Route B
  c. Delivery Route C
  d. Delivery Route D

26. 43 Poway Road
  a. Delivery Route A
  b. Delivery Route B
  c. Delivery Route C
  d. Delivery Route D

27. 644 D Street
  a. Delivery Route A
  b. Delivery Route B
  c. Delivery Route C
  d. Delivery Route D

28. 571 Noyes Ave
  a. Delivery Route A
  b. Delivery Route B
  c. Delivery Route C
  d. Delivery Route D

29. 555 C Street
  a. Delivery Route A
  b. Delivery Route B
  c. Delivery Route C
  d. Delivery Route D

30. 1999 Noyes Ave
  a. Delivery Route A
  b. Delivery Route B
  c. Delivery Route C
  d. Delivery Route D

31. 1299 Jewell Street
  a. Delivery Route A
  b. Delivery Route B
  c. Delivery Route C
  d. Delivery Route D

32. 1100 Noyes Drive
  a. Delivery Route A
  b. Delivery Route B
  c. Delivery Route C
  d. Delivery Route D

33. 352 C Street
  a. Delivery Route A
  b. Delivery Route B
  c. Delivery Route C
  d. Delivery Route D

34. 801 Jewett Street
  a. Delivery Route A
  b. Delivery Route B
  c. Delivery Route C
  d. Delivery Route D

35. 1560 Jewell Street
  a. Delivery Route A
  b. Delivery Route B
  c. Delivery Route C
  d. Delivery Route D

36. 503 C Street
  a. Delivery Route A
  b. Delivery Route B
  c. Delivery Route C
  d. Delivery Route D

Part C, Section 2—Memory

Directions: Spend three minutes memorizing the information found in the **Coding Guide**. You may NOT take any notes during this time. Next, you will answer the 72 questions. Each question offers an **Address**. Choose which **Delivery Route** each address belongs in according to your memory of the Coding Guide. **Note: You may NOT turn back to the page displaying the Coding Guide once the Memory section has begun.**

Time: 3 minutes for memorization, 7 minutes to answer questions

CODING GUIDE	
ADDRESS RANGE	**DELIVERY ROUTE**
700–1300 Jewell Street 1–70 Poway Road 401–600 Noyes Ave	A
201–800 Kettner Drive 99–400 C Street 601–2000 Noyes Ave	B
801–1100 Kettner Drive 499–700 C Street	C
All mail that doesn't belong in one of the address ranges listed here.	D

37. 1002 Kettner Drive
   a. Delivery Route A
   b. Delivery Route B
   c. Delivery Route C
   d. Delivery Route D

38. 44 Poway Road
   a. Delivery Route A
   b. Delivery Route B
   c. Delivery Route C
   d. Delivery Route D

39. 1777 Noyes Ave
   a. Delivery Route A
   b. Delivery Route B
   c. Delivery Route C
   d. Delivery Route D

40. 780 C Street
   a. Delivery Route A
   b. Delivery Route B
   c. Delivery Route C
   d. Delivery Route D

41. 1299 Lowell Street
   a. Delivery Route A
   b. Delivery Route B
   c. Delivery Route C
   d. Delivery Route D

42. 643 C Street
   a. Delivery Route A
   b. Delivery Route B
   c. Delivery Route C
   d. Delivery Route D

43. 1029 Kettner Drive
   a. Delivery Route A
   b. Delivery Route B
   c. Delivery Route C
   d. Delivery Route D

44. 591 C Street
   a. Delivery Route A
   b. Delivery Route B
   c. Delivery Route C
   d. Delivery Route D

45. 785 Kettner Drive
   a. Delivery Route A
   b. Delivery Route B
   c. Delivery Route C
   d. Delivery Route D

46. 49 Powell Road
   a. Delivery Route A
   b. Delivery Route B
   c. Delivery Route C
   d. Delivery Route D

47. 800 Jewell Street
   a. Delivery Route A
   b. Delivery Route B
   c. Delivery Route C
   d. Delivery Route D

48. 679 B Street
   a. Delivery Route A
   b. Delivery Route B
   c. Delivery Route C
   d. Delivery Route D

49. 660 C Street
   a. Delivery Route A
   b. Delivery Route B
   c. Delivery Route C
   d. Delivery Route D

50. 700 Noles Ave
   a. Delivery Route A
   b. Delivery Route B
   c. Delivery Route C
   d. Delivery Route D

51. 938 Kettner Drive
  a. Delivery Route A
  b. Delivery Route B
  c. Delivery Route C
  d. Delivery Route D

52. 771 Jewell Street
  a. Delivery Route A
  b. Delivery Route B
  c. Delivery Route C
  d. Delivery Route D

53. 396 C Street
  a. Delivery Route A
  b. Delivery Route B
  c. Delivery Route C
  d. Delivery Route D

54. 1289 Jewell Street
  a. Delivery Route A
  b. Delivery Route B
  c. Delivery Route C
  d. Delivery Route D

55. 864 Kettner Drive
  a. Delivery Route A
  b. Delivery Route B
  c. Delivery Route C
  d. Delivery Route D

56. 901 Jewell Street
  a. Delivery Route A
  b. Delivery Route B
  c. Delivery Route C
  d. Delivery Route D

57. 113 C Street
  a. Delivery Route A
  b. Delivery Route B
  c. Delivery Route C
  d. Delivery Route D

58. 607 C Street
  a. Delivery Route A
  b. Delivery Route B
  c. Delivery Route C
  d. Delivery Route D

59. 579 Noyes Ave
  a. Delivery Route A
  b. Delivery Route B
  c. Delivery Route C
  d. Delivery Route D

60. 1301 Jewell Street
  a. Delivery Route A
  b. Delivery Route B
  c. Delivery Route C
  d. Delivery Route D

61. 498 Kettner Drive
  a. Delivery Route A
  b. Delivery Route B
  c. Delivery Route C
  d. Delivery Route D

62. 681 C Street
  a. Delivery Route A
  b. Delivery Route B
  c. Delivery Route C
  d. Delivery Route D

63. 8 Poway Drive
  a. Delivery Route A
  b. Delivery Route B
  c. Delivery Route C
  d. Delivery Route D

64. 158 C Street
  a. Delivery Route A
  b. Delivery Route B
  c. Delivery Route C
  d. Delivery Route D

65. 3 Poway Road
    a. Delivery Route A
    b. Delivery Route B
    c. Delivery Route C
    d. Delivery Route D

66. 296 Kettner Drive
    a. Delivery Route A
    b. Delivery Route B
    c. Delivery Route C
    d. Delivery Route D

67. 254 C Street
    a. Delivery Route A
    b. Delivery Route B
    c. Delivery Route C
    d. Delivery Route D

68. 1537 Noyes Ave
    a. Delivery Route A
    b. Delivery Route B
    c. Delivery Route C
    d. Delivery Route D

69. 551 C Street
    a. Delivery Route A
    b. Delivery Route B
    c. Delivery Route C
    d. Delivery Route D

70. 1111 Jewell Street
    a. Delivery Route A
    b. Delivery Route B
    c. Delivery Route C
    d. Delivery Route D

71. 430 Noyes Ave
    a. Delivery Route A
    b. Delivery Route B
    c. Delivery Route C
    d. Delivery Route D

72. 1987 Noyes Ave
    a. Delivery Route A
    b. Delivery Route B
    c. Delivery Route C
    d. Delivery Route D

▶ Answers

Part A—Address Checking

1. b.	**16.** d.	**31.** c.	**46.** b.
2. a.	**17.** b.	**32.** b.	**47.** b.
3. b.	**18.** d.	**33.** d.	**48.** b.
4. c.	**19.** d.	**34.** b.	**49.** d.
5. b.	**20.** a.	**35.** c.	**50.** b.
6. d.	**21.** c.	**36.** b.	**51.** a.
7. d.	**22.** b.	**37.** c.	**52.** c.
8. d.	**23.** a.	**38.** a.	**53.** b.
9. c.	**24.** d.	**39.** d.	**54.** d.
10. d.	**25.** c.	**40.** d.	**55.** c.
11. d.	**26.** b.	**41.** a.	**56.** a.
12. a.	**27.** d.	**42.** d.	**57.** d.
13. d.	**28.** a.	**43.** c.	**58.** a.
14. b.	**29.** a.	**44.** d.	**59.** c.
15. a.	**30.** a.	**45.** c.	**60.** b.

Part B—Forms Completion

1. b. Boxes 7C and 8C both require ZIP codes; therefore, **b** is correct.

2. d. Box A5 requires an expiration date.

3. a. The client type is found in box 1. Because the Gleason company is a business, box 1C should contain a check mark.

4. a. The current street address would be found in box 7.

5. c. Box 4 asks for a business name. If the client type is a business (box 1C is checked), then box 4 must be completed.

6. b. The clerk's name would be found in boxes A3 and A4 where his or her name and signature are required.

7. c. Box 4 requires a business name, not a date.

8. d. Wisconsin is a state, and only two boxes require a state's name as an entry; these are boxes 7B and 8B.

9. b. Box 8C requires a ZIP code; therefore, **b** is correct.

10. d. Box 7 requires an address, not a name.

11. a. Box 2 requires an insurance value. The only choice that shows this is **a**.

12. c. Boxes 1 and 4 require check marks, so the answer is **c**.

13. c. Box 3d requires a name of a country; therefore, **c** is correct.

14. d. Box 4 details whether an item has been delivered. If it has not, box 4b should be checked.

15. b. The recipient's full name and signature are required for this form; therefore, **b** is correct.

16. c. Boxes 5 and 6a both require dates; therefore, **c** is correct.

17. b. The country (Scotland) belongs in box 3d.

18. b. Box 1 asks about the type of item being shipped. In this case, it is a package, so box B should include a check mark.

19. b. Line 5b asks for the day the item is delivered; in this case, it is 13.

20. d. The postmark belongs in box 7.

21. c. A state's name is required for box B2; therefore, **c** is correct.

22. d. Box D requires a date.

23. c. Box G relates to the service provided. If the package arrives bulk rate, then box G3 would include a check mark.

24. b. Box B2 requires a state's name; therefore, **b** is correct.

25. b. Only one name, the recipient's, appears on this form.

26. c. Box F would include the confirmation number.

27. b. The instructions in box G read, "check one." Therefore, **b** is correct.

28. a. Because box B3 requires a ZIP code, only **a** is correct.

29. c. The postmark belongs in box E.

30. d. Two boxes should be checked: the one indicating "under 5 lbs." (C1) and the one indicating an "envelope" (C3).

Part C, Section 1—Coding

1. a.	**10.** c.	**19.** a.	**28.** a.
2. a.	**11.** d.	**20.** c.	**29.** c.
3. d.	**12.** a.	**21.** c.	**30.** b.
4. b.	**13.** c.	**22.** d.	**31.** a.
5. b.	**14.** b.	**23.** a.	**32.** d.
6. c.	**15.** d.	**24.** b.	**33.** b.
7. d.	**16.** d.	**25.** d.	**34.** d.
8. a.	**17.** c.	**26.** a.	**35.** d.
9. b.	**18.** b.	**27.** d.	**36.** c.

Part C, Section 2—Memory

37. c.	**46.** d.	**55.** c.	**64.** b.
38. a.	**47.** a.	**56.** a.	**65.** a.
39. b.	**48.** d.	**57.** b.	**66.** b.
40. d.	**49.** c.	**58.** c.	**67.** b.
41. d.	**50.** d.	**59.** a.	**68.** b.
42. c.	**51.** c.	**60.** d.	**69.** c.
43. c.	**52.** a.	**61.** b.	**70.** a.
44. c.	**53.** b.	**62.** c.	**71.** a.
45. b.	**54.** a.	**63.** d.	**72.** b.

▶ Scoring

As with the other exams in this book, first you must determine your raw score on the exam.

Your Raw Score

Here's how to determine your raw score for each part.

Part A—Address Checking

First, count the questions you got right. Then, count the number of questions you got wrong. Questions you didn't answer don't count either way. Don't forget to multiply the questions you got wrong by $\frac{1}{3}$.

1. Number of questions right: _____
2. Number of questions wrong: _____
3. Number of questions wrong
   multiplied by $\frac{1}{3}$: _____
4. Subtract number 3 from number 1: _____

The result in line 4 is your raw score on Part A.

Part B—Forms Completion

Count the questions you got right. Questions you got wrong or didn't answer don't count either way.

Number of questions right: _____

The result is your raw score on Part B.

Part C, Section 1—Coding

First, count the questions you got right. Then, count the number of questions you got wrong. Questions you didn't answer don't count either way. Don't forget to multiply the questions you got wrong by $\frac{1}{3}$.

1. Number of questions right: _____
2. Number of questions wrong: _____
3. Number of questions wrong
   multiplied by $\frac{1}{3}$: _____
4. Subtract number 3 from number 1: _____

The result in line 4 is your raw score on this section of Part C.

Part C, Section 2—Memory

First, count the questions you got right. Then, count the number of questions you got wrong. Questions you didn't answer don't count either way. Don't forget to multiply the questions you got wrong by $\frac{1}{3}$.

1. Number of questions right: _____
2. Number of questions wrong: _____
3. Number of questions wrong
   multiplied by $\frac{1}{3}$: _____
4. Subtract number 3 from number 1: _____

The result in line 4 is your raw score on this section of Part C.

Part D—Personal Characteristics and Experience Inventory

Remember, there are no right or wrong answers on this section of Test 473 and these questions appear only once in Chapter 8. In addition, the USPS has not released information on how your responses to the questions are "scored." For these reasons, Part D is not used to calculate your raw score on this practice exam.

Total Raw Score

For your total raw score, add together the four raw scores you just calculated.

Total raw score: _____

Basic Rating

To calculate your basic rating, the USPS converts your raw scores on Parts A, B, and C and factors in the results of Part D. As aforementioned, the basic rating is based on a scale of 1 to 100 with 70 being the required passing score to be eligible for a job with the USPS. It is very difficult to give you an accurate basic rating based on this practice exam; however, if your raw score is above 100, you are on your way to passing the official exam.

The Next Step

Hopefully you are continuing to see improvement in your raw scores. If not, you still have another practice exam to hone your test-taking skills. Make sure to continue to review the relevant chapters before you take the next practice exam.

11 ▶ Practice Postal Worker Exam 4

CHAPTER SUMMARY

This is the fourth and final practice exam in this book. You should use it as one of your final steps of preparation for Test 473, the Postal Worker Exam.

Before you start this test, get prepared to simulate the actual test-taking experience as much as possible. Get out your stopwatch or alarm clock so that you can time yourself on each part of the exam. As always, you should have a quiet place to work, some No. 2 pencils, and enough time to complete the test in one sitting—about an hour, including a few minutes of break time between each part.

The answer sheet you should use for answering the questions is on pages 169–170. Then comes the exam itself, and after that is the answer key. The answer key is followed by a section on how to score your exam.

▶ Part A: Address Checking

1.	ⓐ ⓑ ⓒ ⓓ	21.	ⓐ ⓑ ⓒ ⓓ	41.	ⓐ ⓑ ⓒ ⓓ
2.	ⓐ ⓑ ⓒ ⓓ	22.	ⓐ ⓑ ⓒ ⓓ	42.	ⓐ ⓑ ⓒ ⓓ
3.	ⓐ ⓑ ⓒ ⓓ	23.	ⓐ ⓑ ⓒ ⓓ	43.	ⓐ ⓑ ⓒ ⓓ
4.	ⓐ ⓑ ⓒ ⓓ	24.	ⓐ ⓑ ⓒ ⓓ	44.	ⓐ ⓑ ⓒ ⓓ
5.	ⓐ ⓑ ⓒ ⓓ	25.	ⓐ ⓑ ⓒ ⓓ	45.	ⓐ ⓑ ⓒ ⓓ
6.	ⓐ ⓑ ⓒ ⓓ	26.	ⓐ ⓑ ⓒ ⓓ	46.	ⓐ ⓑ ⓒ ⓓ
7.	ⓐ ⓑ ⓒ ⓓ	27.	ⓐ ⓑ ⓒ ⓓ	47.	ⓐ ⓑ ⓒ ⓓ
8.	ⓐ ⓑ ⓒ ⓓ	28.	ⓐ ⓑ ⓒ ⓓ	48.	ⓐ ⓑ ⓒ ⓓ
9.	ⓐ ⓑ ⓒ ⓓ	29.	ⓐ ⓑ ⓒ ⓓ	49.	ⓐ ⓑ ⓒ ⓓ
10.	ⓐ ⓑ ⓒ ⓓ	30.	ⓐ ⓑ ⓒ ⓓ	50.	ⓐ ⓑ ⓒ ⓓ
11.	ⓐ ⓑ ⓒ ⓓ	31.	ⓐ ⓑ ⓒ ⓓ	51.	ⓐ ⓑ ⓒ ⓓ
12.	ⓐ ⓑ ⓒ ⓓ	32.	ⓐ ⓑ ⓒ ⓓ	52.	ⓐ ⓑ ⓒ ⓓ
13.	ⓐ ⓑ ⓒ ⓓ	33.	ⓐ ⓑ ⓒ ⓓ	53.	ⓐ ⓑ ⓒ ⓓ
14.	ⓐ ⓑ ⓒ ⓓ	34.	ⓐ ⓑ ⓒ ⓓ	54.	ⓐ ⓑ ⓒ ⓓ
15.	ⓐ ⓑ ⓒ ⓓ	35.	ⓐ ⓑ ⓒ ⓓ	55.	ⓐ ⓑ ⓒ ⓓ
16.	ⓐ ⓑ ⓒ ⓓ	36.	ⓐ ⓑ ⓒ ⓓ	56.	ⓐ ⓑ ⓒ ⓓ
17.	ⓐ ⓑ ⓒ ⓓ	37.	ⓐ ⓑ ⓒ ⓓ	57.	ⓐ ⓑ ⓒ ⓓ
18.	ⓐ ⓑ ⓒ ⓓ	38.	ⓐ ⓑ ⓒ ⓓ	58.	ⓐ ⓑ ⓒ ⓓ
19.	ⓐ ⓑ ⓒ ⓓ	39.	ⓐ ⓑ ⓒ ⓓ	59.	ⓐ ⓑ ⓒ ⓓ
20.	ⓐ ⓑ ⓒ ⓓ	40.	ⓐ ⓑ ⓒ ⓓ	60.	ⓐ ⓑ ⓒ ⓓ

▶ Part B: Forms Completion

1.	ⓐ ⓑ ⓒ ⓓ	11.	ⓐ ⓑ ⓒ ⓓ	21.	ⓐ ⓑ ⓒ ⓓ
2.	ⓐ ⓑ ⓒ ⓓ	12.	ⓐ ⓑ ⓒ ⓓ	22.	ⓐ ⓑ ⓒ ⓓ
3.	ⓐ ⓑ ⓒ ⓓ	13.	ⓐ ⓑ ⓒ ⓓ	23.	ⓐ ⓑ ⓒ ⓓ
4.	ⓐ ⓑ ⓒ ⓓ	14.	ⓐ ⓑ ⓒ ⓓ	24.	ⓐ ⓑ ⓒ ⓓ
5.	ⓐ ⓑ ⓒ ⓓ	15.	ⓐ ⓑ ⓒ ⓓ	25.	ⓐ ⓑ ⓒ ⓓ
6.	ⓐ ⓑ ⓒ ⓓ	16.	ⓐ ⓑ ⓒ ⓓ	26.	ⓐ ⓑ ⓒ ⓓ
7.	ⓐ ⓑ ⓒ ⓓ	17.	ⓐ ⓑ ⓒ ⓓ	27.	ⓐ ⓑ ⓒ ⓓ
8.	ⓐ ⓑ ⓒ ⓓ	18.	ⓐ ⓑ ⓒ ⓓ	28.	ⓐ ⓑ ⓒ ⓓ
9.	ⓐ ⓑ ⓒ ⓓ	19.	ⓐ ⓑ ⓒ ⓓ	29.	ⓐ ⓑ ⓒ ⓓ
10.	ⓐ ⓑ ⓒ ⓓ	20.	ⓐ ⓑ ⓒ ⓓ	30.	ⓐ ⓑ ⓒ ⓓ

▶ Part C: Section 1–Coding

1.	ⓐ	ⓑ	ⓒ	ⓓ	13.	ⓐ	ⓑ	ⓒ	ⓓ	25.	ⓐ	ⓑ	ⓒ	ⓓ
2.	ⓐ	ⓑ	ⓒ	ⓓ	14.	ⓐ	ⓑ	ⓒ	ⓓ	26.	ⓐ	ⓑ	ⓒ	ⓓ
3.	ⓐ	ⓑ	ⓒ	ⓓ	15.	ⓐ	ⓑ	ⓒ	ⓓ	27.	ⓐ	ⓑ	ⓒ	ⓓ
4.	ⓐ	ⓑ	ⓒ	ⓓ	16.	ⓐ	ⓑ	ⓒ	ⓓ	28.	ⓐ	ⓑ	ⓒ	ⓓ
5.	ⓐ	ⓑ	ⓒ	ⓓ	17.	ⓐ	ⓑ	ⓒ	ⓓ	29.	ⓐ	ⓑ	ⓒ	ⓓ
6.	ⓐ	ⓑ	ⓒ	ⓓ	18.	ⓐ	ⓑ	ⓒ	ⓓ	30.	ⓐ	ⓑ	ⓒ	ⓓ
7.	ⓐ	ⓑ	ⓒ	ⓓ	19.	ⓐ	ⓑ	ⓒ	ⓓ	31.	ⓐ	ⓑ	ⓒ	ⓓ
8.	ⓐ	ⓑ	ⓒ	ⓓ	20.	ⓐ	ⓑ	ⓒ	ⓓ	32.	ⓐ	ⓑ	ⓒ	ⓓ
9.	ⓐ	ⓑ	ⓒ	ⓓ	21.	ⓐ	ⓑ	ⓒ	ⓓ	33.	ⓐ	ⓑ	ⓒ	ⓓ
10.	ⓐ	ⓑ	ⓒ	ⓓ	22.	ⓐ	ⓑ	ⓒ	ⓓ	34.	ⓐ	ⓑ	ⓒ	ⓓ
11.	ⓐ	ⓑ	ⓒ	ⓓ	23.	ⓐ	ⓑ	ⓒ	ⓓ	35.	ⓐ	ⓑ	ⓒ	ⓓ
12.	ⓐ	ⓑ	ⓒ	ⓓ	24.	ⓐ	ⓑ	ⓒ	ⓓ	36.	ⓐ	ⓑ	ⓒ	ⓓ

▶ Part C: Section 2–Memory

37.	ⓐ	ⓑ	ⓒ	ⓓ	49.	ⓐ	ⓑ	ⓒ	ⓓ	61.	ⓐ	ⓑ	ⓒ	ⓓ
38.	ⓐ	ⓑ	ⓒ	ⓓ	50.	ⓐ	ⓑ	ⓒ	ⓓ	62.	ⓐ	ⓑ	ⓒ	ⓓ
39.	ⓐ	ⓑ	ⓒ	ⓓ	51.	ⓐ	ⓑ	ⓒ	ⓓ	63.	ⓐ	ⓑ	ⓒ	ⓓ
40.	ⓐ	ⓑ	ⓒ	ⓓ	52.	ⓐ	ⓑ	ⓒ	ⓓ	64.	ⓐ	ⓑ	ⓒ	ⓓ
41.	ⓐ	ⓑ	ⓒ	ⓓ	53.	ⓐ	ⓑ	ⓒ	ⓓ	65.	ⓐ	ⓑ	ⓒ	ⓓ
42.	ⓐ	ⓑ	ⓒ	ⓓ	54.	ⓐ	ⓑ	ⓒ	ⓓ	66.	ⓐ	ⓑ	ⓒ	ⓓ
43.	ⓐ	ⓑ	ⓒ	ⓓ	55.	ⓐ	ⓑ	ⓒ	ⓓ	67.	ⓐ	ⓑ	ⓒ	ⓓ
44.	ⓐ	ⓑ	ⓒ	ⓓ	56.	ⓐ	ⓑ	ⓒ	ⓓ	68.	ⓐ	ⓑ	ⓒ	ⓓ
45.	ⓐ	ⓑ	ⓒ	ⓓ	57.	ⓐ	ⓑ	ⓒ	ⓓ	69.	ⓐ	ⓑ	ⓒ	ⓓ
46.	ⓐ	ⓑ	ⓒ	ⓓ	58.	ⓐ	ⓑ	ⓒ	ⓓ	70.	ⓐ	ⓑ	ⓒ	ⓓ
47.	ⓐ	ⓑ	ⓒ	ⓓ	59.	ⓐ	ⓑ	ⓒ	ⓓ	71.	ⓐ	ⓑ	ⓒ	ⓓ
48.	ⓐ	ⓑ	ⓒ	ⓓ	60.	ⓐ	ⓑ	ⓒ	ⓓ	72.	ⓐ	ⓑ	ⓒ	ⓓ

▶ Practice Postal Worker Exam 4

Part A—Address Checking

Directions: Review and compare the information in the **List to Be Checked** with the information in the **Correct List**. To answer each question, you must decide if there are **No errors (a)**, an error in the **Address only (b)**, an error in the **ZIP code only (c)**, or an error in **Both (d)** the address and the ZIP code. This part has 60 questions.

Time: 11 minutes

	CORRECT LIST		LIST TO BE CHECKED	
QUESTION	**ADDRESS**	**ZIP CODE**	**ADDRESS**	**ZIP CODE**
1.	1254 Oakley Ave Highlands, TX	77562-0937	1254 Oakley Ave Highlands, TX	77562-0997
2.	7661 Friars Road Elk Park, NC	28622	7661 N Friars Road Elk Park, ND	28622
3.	9000 Mission Gorge Avenue Atglen, PA	19310	9009 Mission Gorge Avenue Atglen, PA	19310
4.	1523 May Dr Gobler, MO	63849	1523 Mey Dr Gobler, MO	63849
5.	835 Truman Ln Lucedale, MS	39452	835 Truman Ln Lucedale, MS	39542
6.	2345 Erzen Drive Numa, IA	52544	2345 E Zen Drive Numa, IA	52544
7.	9853 Nolan Cir Port Henry, NY	12974-6842	93 Nolan Cir Port Henry, NY	12974-6482
8.	12 W Fourth Ave Slab Fork, WV	25920-7254	123 Fourth Ave Slab Fork, WV	52920-7254
9.	763 Northern Road Miracle, KY	40856	763 Northern Road Miracle, KS	40856
10.	3334 Convoy St Clayton, NJ	08312	3334 Convoy St Clayton, NJ	08312
11.	5674 Arena Boulevard Hiawatha, IA	52233	5674 Arena Boulevard Hiawatha, IA	52333

a. No errors
b. Address only
c. ZIP code only
d. Both

QUESTION	CORRECT LIST ADDRESS	ZIP CODE	LIST TO BE CHECKED ADDRESS	ZIP CODE
12.	987 Chantilly Way Benge, WA	99105	987 Chantilly Way Benge, WA	91105
13.	3411 7th Street La Luz, NM	88337-2846	3411 7th Street La Luz, NM	80337-2846
14.	PO Box 87402 Kimberly, OR	97848	PO Box 87402 Kimberly, OK	97888
15.	5472 Brasco Dr Perryville, AK	99648	5472 Brasco Dr Perryton, AK	99648
16.	441 Raven Avenue Skok, WA	98584	441 Raven Avenue Skokie, WA	98584
17.	6084 Sonnet Road West Lima, WI	54639	6084 Sonnet Road West Lima, WI	54639
18.	1231 McGregor St Mason, NH	03048-2759	1231 McGregor St Mason, NH	03048-2779
19.	11 9th Ave S Flippin, AR	72634	11 9th Ave Flippin, AR	72643
20.	87 Tustin Street Harlem, MT	59526	87 Tustin Street Harlem, MI	59566
21.	68 Seagull Way Milwaukee, WI	53259	68 Seagull Way Milwaukee, WI	53259
22.	5378 Rommen Avenue Saint Elmo, IL	36568-0909	5378 Romman Avenue Saint Elmo, IL	36568-0900
23.	PO Box 44479 Milan, OH	44846	PO Box 44479 Milan, OK	48846
24.	924 Komen Road Fola, WV	25019	924 Komen Road Fola, WA	25019
25.	46343 Hobbing Drive Fork, MD	21051	46343 Hobbi Drive Fork, MD	21501
26.	932 Rosemary Lane Honomu, HI	96728	392 Rosemary Lane Honomu, HI	96728

a. No errors
b. Address only
c. ZIP code only
d. Both

	CORRECT LIST		LIST TO BE CHECKED	
QUESTION	ADDRESS	ZIP CODE	ADDRESS	ZIP CODE
27.	222 Arco Boulevard Cee Vee, TX	79223-7000	223 Arco Boulevard Cee Vee, TX	79223-7009
28.	631 Pennington Way Chandler, OK	74834	661 Rennington Way Chandler, OK	74844
29.	875 Kinsey Dr Formoso, KS	66942	875 Kinsey Dr Formoso, KY	69642
30.	6812 Bradford Cir Herkimer, NY	13350-5392	6812 Branford Cir Herkimer, NY	11350-5392
31.	3645 Tylo Road Dulzura, CA	91917	3645 Tylo Road Dulzura, CA	91911
32.	487 Spring St Sagle, ID	83860	487 Spring St Sagle, ID	83866
33.	2574 Holton Cir Kealakekua, HI	96750	2574 Holton Cir Kealakekua, HI	96750
34.	PO Box 93765 Mio, MI	48647	PO Box 93765 Mio, MS	48647
35.	78 River Street Ravenna, TX	75476	78 River Road Ravenna, TX	75476
36.	4567 Clark Boulevard Tacoma, WA	98439-5532	4567 Clark Boulevard Tacoma, WA	89439-5532
37.	97 Elgin Way Welcome, MD	20693-6521	97 Elgin Way Welcome, MA	20693-6521
38.	3673 Mermin Road Red Oak, GA	30272-0943	3673 Mirmin Road Red Oak, CA	32072-0943
39.	3 Apollo Street Obert, NE	68757	31 Apollo Street Obert, NE	68757
40.	122 Champagne Ln Helper, UT	84526	121 Champagne Ln Helper, UT	84562
41.	54 Walter Circle Cocolalla, ID	83813	54 Walter Circle Cocolalla, IA	88813

a. No errors

b. Address only

c. ZIP code only

d. Both

QUESTION	CORRECT LIST ADDRESS	ZIP CODE	LIST TO BE CHECKED ADDRESS	ZIP CODE
42.	745 Sawyer Boulevard Allen, SD	57714-7254	745 Sawyer Boulevard Allen, SD	51714-7254
43.	4575 Yorin St Olton, TX	79064	4775 Yorin St Olton, TX	79604
44.	76 8th Ave N Alcova, WY	82620	76 8th Ave S Alcova, WY	82620
45.	34 West St Clay, AL	35048	340 West St Clay, AL	35084
46.	5402 Minder Ave Beauty, KY	41203	5042 Minder Ave Beauty, KY	41203
47.	333 State Boulevard Baxter, WV	26560	330 State Boulevard Baxter, WV	26560
48.	PO Box 53200 Iliff, CO	80736	PO Box 53200 Iliff, CO	80736
49.	7546 Aaron Ln Polk, OH	44866	7546 Aaron Ln Polk, OH	48866
50.	983 S Olin Dr Flying H, NM	88339	983 S Olin Dr Flying H, NM	88339
51.	3411 Fontana Road Cairo, IL	62914-9364	3411 Fontana Road Cairo, IL	62994-9364
52.	67 Rutgen Ave Mc Fall, MO	64657-3522	67 Rutgers Ave Mc Fall, MO	64657-3522
53.	31 Montana Dr Nulato, AK	99765-4665	311 Montana Dr Nulato, AK	99765-4655
54.	4555 Grawn Street Rye, CO	81069	4555 Grown Street Rye, CO	81096
55.	14 Sixth St Sneads, FL	32460	14 Sixth St Sneads, FL	32640
56.	7221 Collins Dr Venia, VA	24260-9463	7221 Collins Dr Venia, VA	24260-9463

a. No errors
b. Address only
c. ZIP code only
d. Both

	CORRECT LIST		LIST TO BE CHECKED	
QUESTION	**ADDRESS**	**ZIP CODE**	**ADDRESS**	**ZIP CODE**
57.	PO Box 25367 Wick, WV	26149	PO Box 25367 Wick, WV	26649
58.	96734 Everton Way Pevely, MO	63070-5834	96734 Everton Way Pevely, MS	63070-5834
59.	45 10th Street Florida, MA	01247	95 10th Street Florida, MA	01247
60.	600 Polanis Dr Why, AZ	85321	600 Polanis Dr Why, AZ	83321

a. No errors
b. Address only
c. ZIP code only
d. Both

Part B—Forms Completion

Directions: Review each form and answer the 30 questions that follow.

Time: 15 minutes

Redirected Mail Form

1. Last Name	2. First Name	
3. Current Address		
3A. Current City	3B. Current State	3C. Current ZIP Code
4. Date to Redirect 4A. Day 4B. Mo. 4C. Year	1A. Zone	
	1B. Route Number	
5. Type of Mail (check all that apply) 5A. [ ] Letters 5C. [ ] Magazines 5B. [ ] Packages 5D. [ ] Other	1C. Clerk ID Number	
	1D. Clerk's Signature	
6. Redirected Address	1E. Postmark	
6A. Redirected City		
6B. Redirected State	6C. Redirected ZIP Code	

1. If mail is to be redirected in 2009, on which line would you find this information?
a. 4
b. 4A
c. 4B
d. 4C

2. Where does the new address belong?
a. box 3
b. box 1A
c. box 3C
d. box 6

3. How many ZIP codes are required to complete this form?
a. 0
b. 1
c. 2
d. 3

4. If mail is being redirected to Los Angeles, where should this information be entered?
a. box 3
b. box 3A
c. box 6
d. box 6A

5. What information belongs in box 1A?
   a. zone
   b. route number
   c. clerk ID number
   d. redirected ZIP code

6. If box 5C is checked, what type of mail will be redirected?
   a. letters
   b. packages
   c. magazines
   d. other

7. The information "8742 Long Shore Dr" would be a reasonable entry for which box?
   a. 3A
   b. 3C
   c. 5
   d. 6

8. What box should contain a signature?
   a. 1
   b. 2
   c. 1D
   d. 1E

9. If someone is moving from California to Hawaii, where should he or she enter "Hawaii"?
   a. box 3B
   b. box 6B
   c. box 3C
   d. box 1E

10. If all types of mail should be redirected, how many boxes would be checked in box 5?
   a. 1
   b. 2
   c. 3
   d. 4

Receipt

1a. Name	
1b. Address	
1c. City	1d. State
1e. ZIP Code	1f. +4 ZIP Code
2. Postage $	3. Certification Fee $
4. Total Postage and Fees $	
5. Signature	6. Date

11. Where does the current date belong?
   a. box 1d
   b. box 2
   c. box 4
   d. box 6

12. In which box would you enter +4059?
   a. box 1d
   b. box 1e
   c. box 1f
   d. box 1g

13. The information "$40.80" is a reasonable entry for which of the following boxes?
   a. 1e
   b. 1f
   c. 2
   d. 5

14. If the certification fee is $2.70, where should this information be entered?
   a. box 3
   b. box 4
   c. box 5
   d. box 6

15. Which of the following belongs in box 1e?
   a. Providence
   b. Rhode Island
   c. 02904
   d. +4 ZIP code

16. The state name belongs in which of the following?
   a. 1d
   b. 1e
   c. 2
   d. 6

17. If just the postage is $4.90, where should this amount be entered?

a. 2

b. 3

c. 4

d. 6

18. Which of the following would be an appropriate entry for box 4?

a. 40320

b. 4/23/2009

c. $40.32

d. 4032 Oster St

19. In which box would "New York City" be an entry?

a. 1b

b. 1c

c. 1d

d. 1f

20. Where should a signature appear?

a. 5

b. 6

c. 1a

d. 1b

Certificate of Mailing

A. Sender's Name		
B. Sender's Address		
B1. Sender's City	B2. State	B2. ZIP Code
C. Recipient's Name		
D. Recipient's Address		
D1. Recipient's City	D2. State	D3. ZIP Code
E. Sender's Signature	E1. Date	
F. All Stamps to Be Affixed in This Box ONLY.		

21. Stamps should only appear in which box?

a. D3

b. E

c. E1

d. F

22. Which of the following would be an entry for box E1?

a. Nevada

b. 11373

c. 1/24/09

d. signature

23. How many ZIP codes would complete this form?
   a. 0
   b. 1
   c. 2
   d. 3

24. The information "55736" would be an appropriate entry for which box?
   a. B1
   b. B3
   c. D1
   d. D2

25. How many different names should appear on this form?
   a. 1
   b. 2
   c. 3
   d. none

26. The sender's address belongs in
   a. box A
   b. box B
   c. box D
   d. box E

27. If the recipient lives in North Dakota, where would this be indicated?
   a. box D
   b. box D1
   c. box D2
   d. box F

28. City names belong in which of the following boxes?
   a. B1 only
   b. D1 only
   c. B1 and D1
   d. D3

29. "Kansas" would be an appropriate entry for which of these boxes?
   a. B
   b. D2
   c. D1
   d. D3

30. The sender must sign which of the following boxes?
   a. A
   b. C
   c. E
   d. F

Part C, Section 1—Coding

Directions: Read and review the **Coding Guide**. Each of the 26 questions offers an **Address**. Choose which **Delivery Route** each address belongs in according to the Coding Guide.

Time: 6 minutes

CODING GUIDE	
ADDRESS RANGE	**DELIVERY ROUTE**
1–199 Dennison Street 400–699 4th Street 10–299 Village Drive	A
800–3600 Herschel Drive 10–40 Route 7 200–800 Dennison Street	B
300–399 Village Drive 800–999 4th Street	C
All mail that doesn't belong in one of the address ranges listed here.	D

1. 15 Dennison Street
   a. Delivery Route A
   b. Delivery Route B
   c. Delivery Route C
   d. Delivery Route D

2. 11 Route 7
   a. Delivery Route A
   b. Delivery Route B
   c. Delivery Route C
   d. Delivery Route D

3. 11 Route 17
   a. Delivery Route A
   b. Delivery Route B
   c. Delivery Route C
   d. Delivery Route D

4. 980 Herschel Drive
   a. Delivery Route A
   b. Delivery Route B
   c. Delivery Route C
   d. Delivery Route D

5. 456 4th Street
   a. Delivery Route A
   b. Delivery Route B
   c. Delivery Route C
   d. Delivery Route D

6. 457 14th Street
   a. Delivery Route A
   b. Delivery Route B
   c. Delivery Route C
   d. Delivery Route D

7. 321 Village Drive
  a. Delivery Route A
  b. Delivery Route B
  c. Delivery Route C
  d. Delivery Route D

8. 873 4th Street
  a. Delivery Route A
  b. Delivery Route B
  c. Delivery Route C
  d. Delivery Route D

9. 17 Route 7
  a. Delivery Route A
  b. Delivery Route B
  c. Delivery Route C
  d. Delivery Route D

10. 3111 Herschel Drive
  a. Delivery Route A
  b. Delivery Route B
  c. Delivery Route C
  d. Delivery Route D

11. 74 Dennison Street
  a. Delivery Route A
  b. Delivery Route B
  c. Delivery Route C
  d. Delivery Route D

12. 233 Village Drive
  a. Delivery Route A
  b. Delivery Route B
  c. Delivery Route C
  d. Delivery Route D

13. 512 4th Street
  a. Delivery Route A
  b. Delivery Route B
  c. Delivery Route C
  d. Delivery Route D

14. 322 Village Drive
  a. Delivery Route A
  b. Delivery Route B
  c. Delivery Route C
  d. Delivery Route D

15. 444 45th Street
  a. Delivery Route A
  b. Delivery Route B
  c. Delivery Route C
  d. Delivery Route D

16. 799 Herschel Drive
  a. Delivery Route A
  b. Delivery Route B
  c. Delivery Route C
  d. Delivery Route D

17. 201 Dennison Street
  a. Delivery Route A
  b. Delivery Route B
  c. Delivery Route C
  d. Delivery Route D

18. 904 4th Street
  a. Delivery Route A
  b. Delivery Route B
  c. Delivery Route C
  d. Delivery Route D

19. 34 Route 7
  a. Delivery Route A
  b. Delivery Route B
  c. Delivery Route C
  d. Delivery Route D

20. 3440 Herschel Road
  a. Delivery Route A
  b. Delivery Route B
  c. Delivery Route C
  d. Delivery Route D

21. 1 Route 7
    a. Delivery Route A
    b. Delivery Route B
    c. Delivery Route C
    d. Delivery Route D

22. 974 Herschel Drive
    a. Delivery Route A
    b. Delivery Route B
    c. Delivery Route C
    d. Delivery Route D

23. 499 4th Street
    a. Delivery Route A
    b. Delivery Route B
    c. Delivery Route C
    d. Delivery Route D

24. 303 Village Drive
    a. Delivery Route A
    b. Delivery Route B
    c. Delivery Route C
    d. Delivery Route D

25. 804 4th Street
    a. Delivery Route A
    b. Delivery Route B
    c. Delivery Route C
    d. Delivery Route D

26. 3800 Herschel Drive
    a. Delivery Route A
    b. Delivery Route B
    c. Delivery Route C
    d. Delivery Route D

27. 314 Village Drive
    a. Delivery Route A
    b. Delivery Route B
    c. Delivery Route C
    d. Delivery Route D

28. 8 Denison Street
    a. Delivery Route A
    b. Delivery Route B
    c. Delivery Route C
    d. Delivery Route D

29. 928 4th Street
    a. Delivery Route A
    b. Delivery Route B
    c. Delivery Route C
    d. Delivery Route D

30. 22 Route 7
    a. Delivery Route A
    b. Delivery Route B
    c. Delivery Route C
    d. Delivery Route D

31. 1490 Herschel Drive
    a. Delivery Route A
    b. Delivery Route B
    c. Delivery Route C
    d. Delivery Route D

32. 89 Dennison Street
    a. Delivery Route A
    b. Delivery Route B
    c. Delivery Route C
    d. Delivery Route D

33. 398 Village Drive
    a. Delivery Route A
    b. Delivery Route B
    c. Delivery Route C
    d. Delivery Route D

34. 89 Route 7
    a. Delivery Route A
    b. Delivery Route B
    c. Delivery Route C
    d. Delivery Route D

35. 881 4th Street
    a. Delivery Route A
    b. Delivery Route B
    c. Delivery Route C
    d. Delivery Route D

36. 299 Village Drive
    a. Delivery Route A
    b. Delivery Route B
    c. Delivery Route C
    d. Delivery Route D

Part C, Section 2—Memory

Directions: Spend three minutes memorizing the information found in the **Coding Guide**. You may NOT take any notes during this time. Next, you will answer the 72 questions. Each question offers an **Address**. Choose which **Delivery Route** each address belongs in according to your memory of the Coding Guide. **Note: You may NOT turn back to the page displaying the Coding Guide once the Memory section has begun.**

Time: 3 minutes for memorization, 7 minutes to answer questions

CODING GUIDE	
ADDRESS RANGE	**DELIVERY ROUTE**
1–199 Dennison Street 400–699 4th Street 10–299 Village Drive	A
800–3600 Herschel Drive 10–40 Route 7 200–800 Dennison Street	B
300–399 Village Drive 800–999 4th Street	C
All mail that doesn't belong in one of the address ranges listed here.	D

37. 399 Dennison Street
   a. Delivery Route A
   b. Delivery Route B
   c. Delivery Route C
   d. Delivery Route D

38. 577 4th Street
   a. Delivery Route A
   b. Delivery Route B
   c. Delivery Route C
   d. Delivery Route D

39. 356 Village Drive
   a. Delivery Route A
   b. Delivery Route B
   c. Delivery Route C
   d. Delivery Route D

40. 17 Route 71
   a. Delivery Route A
   b. Delivery Route B
   c. Delivery Route C
   d. Delivery Route D

41. 77 Dennison Street
   a. Delivery Route A
   b. Delivery Route B
   c. Delivery Route C
   d. Delivery Route D

42. 232 4th Street
   a. Delivery Route A
   b. Delivery Route B
   c. Delivery Route C
   d. Delivery Route D

43. 3573 Herschel Drive
   a. Delivery Route A
   b. Delivery Route B
   c. Delivery Route C
   d. Delivery Route D

44. 217 Village Drive
   a. Delivery Route A
   b. Delivery Route B
   c. Delivery Route C
   d. Delivery Route D

45. 804 4th Street
   a. Delivery Route A
   b. Delivery Route B
   c. Delivery Route C
   d. Delivery Route D

46. 3430 Hershell Drive
   a. Delivery Route A
   b. Delivery Route B
   c. Delivery Route C
   d. Delivery Route D

47. 1100 Dennison Street
   a. Delivery Route A
   b. Delivery Route B
   c. Delivery Route C
   d. Delivery Route D

48. 369 Village Drive
   a. Delivery Route A
   b. Delivery Route B
   c. Delivery Route C
   d. Delivery Route D

49. 999 4th Street
   a. Delivery Route A
   b. Delivery Route B
   c. Delivery Route C
   d. Delivery Route D

50. 760 Dennison Avenue
   a. Delivery Route A
   b. Delivery Route B
   c. Delivery Route C
   d. Delivery Route D

51. 844 4th Street
   a. Delivery Route A
   b. Delivery Route B
   c. Delivery Route C
   d. Delivery Route D

52. 27 Route 7
   a. Delivery Route A
   b. Delivery Route B
   c. Delivery Route C
   d. Delivery Route D

53. 555 4th Avenue
   a. Delivery Route A
   b. Delivery Route B
   c. Delivery Route C
   d. Delivery Route D

54. 378 Village Drive
   a. Delivery Route A
   b. Delivery Route B
   c. Delivery Route C
   d. Delivery Route D

55. 888 Herschel Drive
   a. Delivery Route A
   b. Delivery Route B
   c. Delivery Route C
   d. Delivery Route D

56. 400 4th Street
   a. Delivery Route A
   b. Delivery Route B
   c. Delivery Route C
   d. Delivery Route D

57. 134 Dennison Street
   a. Delivery Route A
   b. Delivery Route B
   c. Delivery Route C
   d. Delivery Route D

58. 173 Dennis Street
   a. Delivery Route A
   b. Delivery Route B
   c. Delivery Route C
   d. Delivery Route D

59. 801 4th Street
   a. Delivery Route A
   b. Delivery Route B
   c. Delivery Route C
   d. Delivery Route D

60. 11 Village Drive
   a. Delivery Route A
   b. Delivery Route B
   c. Delivery Route C
   d. Delivery Route D

61. 33 Route 7
   a. Delivery Route A
   b. Delivery Route B
   c. Delivery Route C
   d. Delivery Route D

62. 541 5th Street
   a. Delivery Route A
   b. Delivery Route B
   c. Delivery Route C
   d. Delivery Route D

63. 641 4th Street
   a. Delivery Route A
   b. Delivery Route B
   c. Delivery Route C
   d. Delivery Route D

64. 501 Dennison Street
   a. Delivery Route A
   b. Delivery Route B
   c. Delivery Route C
   d. Delivery Route D

65. 376 Village Drive
   a. Delivery Route A
   b. Delivery Route B
   c. Delivery Route C
   d. Delivery Route D

66. 555 4th Street
   a. Delivery Route A
   b. Delivery Route B
   c. Delivery Route C
   d. Delivery Route D

67. 563 Dennison Street
   a. Delivery Route A
   b. Delivery Route B
   c. Delivery Route C
   d. Delivery Route D

68. 837 Herschel Blvd.
   a. Delivery Route A
   b. Delivery Route B
   c. Delivery Route C
   d. Delivery Route D

69. 187 Village Drive
   a. Delivery Route A
   b. Delivery Route B
   c. Delivery Route C
   d. Delivery Route D

70. 4 Dennison Street
   a. Delivery Route A
   b. Delivery Route B
   c. Delivery Route C
   d. Delivery Route D

71. 39 Route 7
   a. Delivery Route A
   b. Delivery Route B
   c. Delivery Route C
   d. Delivery Route D

72. 3333 Herschel Drive
   a. Delivery Route A
   b. Delivery Route B
   c. Delivery Route C
   d. Delivery Route D

▶ Answers

Part A—Address Checking

1. c.	**16.** b.	**31.** c.	**46.** b.
2. b.	**17.** a.	**32.** c.	**47.** b.
3. b.	**18.** c.	**33.** a.	**48.** a.
4. b.	**19.** d.	**34.** b.	**49.** c.
5. c.	**20.** d.	**35.** b.	**50.** a.
6. b.	**21.** a.	**36.** c.	**51.** c.
7. d.	**22.** d.	**37.** b.	**52.** b.
8. d.	**23.** d.	**38.** d.	**53.** d.
9. b.	**24.** b.	**39.** b.	**54.** d.
10. a.	**25.** d.	**40.** d.	**55.** c.
11. c.	**26.** b.	**41.** d.	**56.** a.
12. c.	**27.** d.	**42.** c.	**57.** c.
13. c.	**28.** d.	**43.** d.	**58.** b.
14. d.	**29.** d.	**44.** b.	**59.** b.
15. b.	**30.** d.	**45.** d.	**60.** c.

Part B—Forms Completion

1. d. Box 4 includes information on when mail is to be redirected. Line 4C indicates the year.

2. d. The new, or redirected, address belongs in box 6.

3. c. Two ZIP codes complete this form: one for the current address and one for the redirected address.

4. d. If Los Angeles is the redirected city, this information belongs in box 6A.

5. a. Box 1A includes the zone.

6. c. A check mark in box 5C indicates that only magazines will be redirected.

7. d. Of the choices listed, only box 6 requires an address.

8. c. Box 1D includes the clerk's signature.

9. b. Hawaii is the redirected state; therefore, this information belongs in box 6B.

10. d. To indicate that all types of mail should be redirected, all four boxes in box 5 should be checked.

11. d. The current date belongs in box 6.

12. c. The +4 ZIP code belongs in box 1f.

13. c. Of the choices listed, only one, box 2, requires a dollar amount.

14. a. The certification fee belongs in box 3.

15. c. Box 1e requires the ZIP code (02904).

16. a. The state name belongs in box 1d.

17. a. The postage belongs in box 2.

18. c. Box 4 requires the total dollar amount of postage and fees; therefore, **c** is correct.

19. b. Only box 1e requires a city's name; therefore, **b** is correct.

20. a. The signature belongs in box 5.

21. d. According to the form, stamps should only appear in box F.

22. c. Box E1 requires a date (1/24/09).

23. c. Boxes B3 and D3 require ZIP codes; therefore, **c** is correct.

24. b. "55736"is a standard ZIP code. Among the choices, only box B3 requires a ZIP code.

25. b. Only two different names should appear on this form: the sender's name and the recipient's name.

26. b. The sender's address belongs in box B.

27. c. The recipient's state is found in box D2.

28. c. The names of cities belong in boxes B1 and D1.

29. b. Among the choices, only box D2 requires a state's name.

30. c. The sender's signature belongs in box E.

Part C, Section 1—Coding

1. a.	**10.** b.	**19.** b.	**28.** d.
2. b.	**11.** a.	**20.** d.	**29.** c.
3. d.	**12.** a.	**21.** d.	**30.** b.
4. b.	**13.** a.	**22.** b.	**31.** b.
5. a.	**14.** c.	**23.** a.	**32.** a.
6. d.	**15.** d.	**24.** c.	**33.** c.
7. c.	**16.** d.	**25.** c.	**34.** d.
8. c.	**17.** b.	**26.** d.	**35.** c.
9. b.	**18.** c.	**27.** c.	**36.** a.

Part C, Section 2—Memory

37. b.	**46.** d.	**55.** b.	**64.** b.
38. a.	**47.** d.	**56.** a.	**65.** c.
39. c.	**48.** c.	**57.** a.	**66.** a.
40. d.	**49.** c.	**58.** d.	**67.** b.
41. a.	**50.** d.	**59.** c.	**68.** d.
42. d.	**51.** c.	**60.** a.	**69.** a.
43. b.	**52.** b.	**61.** b.	**70.** a.
44. a.	**53.** d.	**62.** d.	**71.** b.
45. c.	**54.** c.	**63.** a.	**72.** b.

► Scoring

As with the other exams in this book, first you must determine your raw score on the exam.

Your Raw Score
Here's how to determine your raw score for each part.

Part A—Address Checking

First, count the questions you got right. Then, count the number of questions you got wrong. Questions you didn't answer don't count either way. Don't forget to multiply the questions you got wrong by $\frac{1}{3}$.

1. Number of questions right: _____
2. Number of questions wrong: _____
3. Number of questions wrong
   multiplied by $\frac{1}{3}$:   _____
4. Subtract number 3 from number 1:   _____

The result in line 4 is your raw score on Part A.

Part B—Forms Completion

Count the questions you got right. Questions you got wrong or didn't answer don't count either way.

Number of questions right: _____

The result is your raw score on Part B.

Part C, Section 1—Coding

First, count the questions you got right. Then, count the number of questions you got wrong. Questions you didn't answer don't count either way. Don't forget to multiply the questions you got wrong by $\frac{1}{3}$.

1. Number of questions right: _____
2. Number of questions wrong: _____
3. Number of questions wrong
   multiplied by $\frac{1}{3}$:   _____
4. Subtract number 3 from number 1:   _____

The result in line 4 is your raw score on this section of Part C.

Part C, Section 2—Memory

First, count the questions you got right. Then, count the number of questions you got wrong. Questions you didn't answer don't count either way. Don't forget to multiply the questions you got wrong by $\frac{1}{3}$.

1. Number of questions right: _____
2. Number of questions wrong: _____
3. Number of questions wrong
   multiplied by $\frac{1}{3}$:   _____
4. Subtract number 3 from number 1:   _____

The result in line 4 is your raw score on this section of Part C.

Part D—Personal Characteristics and Experience Inventory

Remember, there are no right or wrong answers on this section of Test 473 and these questions appear only once in Chapter 8. In addition, the USPS has not released information on how your responses to the questions are "scored." For these reasons, Part D is not used to calculate your raw score on this practice exam.

Total Raw Score

For your total raw score, add together the four raw scores you just calculated.

Total raw score: _____

Basic Rating

To calculate your basic rating, the USPS converts your raw scores on **Parts A**, **B**, and **C** and factors in the results of **Part D**. As aforementioned, the basic rating is based on a scale of 1 to 100 with 70 being the required passing score to be eligible for a job with the USPS. It is very difficult to give you an accurate basic rating based on this practice exam; however, if your raw score is above 100, you are on your way to passing the official exam.

The Next Step

Congratulations! You have completed all four practice exams in this book. You should continue to review any materials about which you still feel unsure. Then, it's time to use the strategies and knowledge that you gained from this book and apply them on test day. Good luck!

NOTES

NOTES

NOTES

NOTES

NOTES